TAE KWON DO

by Thomas Buckley

Content Adviser: Philip S. Porter, Founder,
United States Martial Arts Association,
Citrus Heights, California

The Child's World®

Published in the United States of America by The Child's World®
PO Box 326 • Chanhassen, MN 55317-0326 • 800-599-READ • www.childsworld.com

ACKNOWLEDGMENTS

The Child's World®: Mary Berendes, Publishing Director

Editorial Directions, Inc.: E. Russell Primm, Editorial Director; Halley Gatenby, Line Editor; Susan Hindman, Copyeditor; Elizabeth K. Martin and Katie Marsico, Assistant Editors; Matthew Messbarger, Editorial Assistant; Kerry Reid, Fact Checker; Tim Griffin/IndexServ, Indexer; James Buckley Jr., Photo Researcher and Photo Selector

The Design Lab: Kathleen Petelinsek, Design and Page Production

PHOTOS

Cover: John Henley/Corbis
TRBfoto/Photodisc, 1
AP/Wide World: 8, 12, 14, 18, 19, 25, 27
George Shelley/Corbis: 16
Getty Images: 5, 7, 9, 11, 26, 28
Lisa M McGeady/Corbis: 10
Reuters NewMedia Inc./Corbis: 15
Rick Gomez/Corbis: 21
Tom Stewart/Corbis: 22

REGISTRATION

LIBRARY OF CONGRESS CATALOGING-IN-PUBLICATION DATA

Buckley, Thomas J.
  Tae kwon do / by Thomas Buckley.
    v. cm. — (Kids' guides)
Contents: An ancient and modern fighting style—Forms, sparring, and breaking boards—The art of punching and kicking, and more kicking—Etiquette, respect, and self-control—Self-defense.
  ISBN 1-59296-031-6 (Library Bound : alk. paper)
  1. Tae kwon do—Juvenile literature. [1. Tae kwon do.] I. Title. II. Series.
  GV1114.9.B83 2004
  796.815'3—dc22   2003018080

CONTENTS

THE MOST POPULAR MARTIAL ART

THE KOREAN MARTIAL ART OF TAE KWON DO

is probably one of the most popular and widely practiced martial arts in the world. Tae kwon do means "the way of kicking and punching."

It is an exciting style of high, acrobatic kicks and spinning moves. It features awe-inspiring demonstrations of board and brick breaking. Its **sparring** competitions have become part of the Olympic Games. Tae kwon do is taught all over the world, probably to more students than are taught karate, kung fu, or judo.

Although it is based on ancient Korean fighting techniques, modern tae kwon do is younger than the other fighting styles. For various reasons, martial arts were not taught at all in Korea for many years. It was only after World War II that Korean martial arts training developed into modern tae kwon do. World War II might seem like a long time ago. But kung fu and karate have been developing for hundreds—even thousands—of years.

In spite of its youth, tae kwon do has taken its exciting, high-kicking style to the heights of popularity. Chances are, if there is only one martial arts school in your town, it is a tae kwon do **dojang** (school). Tae kwon do has taken the martial arts world by storm!

Tae kwon do is a relatively new martial art—but has become extremely popular.

4

AN ANCIENT AND MODERN STYLE

THE FIGHTING METHODS THAT LATER

became tae kwon do were probably taught in Korea for many centuries. Scholars have found paintings and sculptures of men in martial arts poses similar to those used in tae kwon do in ancient temples. Some of those paintings and sculptures were created more than 1,500 years ago!

In ancient times, Korea was a warlike place. In about 2300 B.C., the legendary warrior king Tangun (whose name means "the holy warrior") first founded the country, located on a peninsula between China and Japan. He unified the warring tribes there, and his **dynasty** lasted nearly 1,200 years.

After the fall of that dynasty, the land split into three kingdoms: Koguryo, Paekche, and Silla. The tribes of the three kingdoms were constantly at war, and the smallest kingdom, Silla, was constantly under attack. King Jin Heung of Silla developed a powerful force of fighters to defend the kingdom. They were known as the *Hwarangdo*, which means "the way of flowering manhood." The Hwarangdo were respected for their great bravery and skill at combat, even though many of them were still in their teens.

The Hwarangdo knights practiced a dangerous form of unarmed combat known as *soo bakh*. They climbed rugged

Tae kwon do is characterized by its exciting—and sometimes high-flying—kicks.

mountains and waded in icy cold streams to strengthen their bodies. They became a terrific fighting force. These knights led Silla in conquering the other kingdoms and uniting the entire Korean peninsula.

The military leaders of Silla performed demonstrations of soo bakh, which spread its popularity throughout the kingdom. Eventually, soo bakh was practiced throughout the land. Other schools taught styles called *kwon-bup* and *tae kwon*.

As the rule of the Silla kings led to peaceful times, the popularity of martial arts in Korea declined. The years of the Yi dynasty, from 1392 to 1910, were **tranquil.** Military leaders became less important, and the study of martial arts became even less popular.

In 1910, the Japanese conquered Korea, and the practice of martial arts was banned. It would be decades before they were practiced again. In 1943, near the end of World War II, karate (from Okinawa) and judo (from Japan) were introduced.

Little kids all over the United States have fun with and learn from the martial arts.

Proper balance is a critical element to tae kwon do.

Then in 1945, the Koreans were freed from Japan's rule, and the people became very patriotic. As a result, they soon became interested in traditional Korean martial arts like soo bakh and tae kwon.

Chung Do Kwan, the first modern Korean dojang, was built in 1945. A few years later, the president of Korea ordered all of its soldiers and military forces to study the traditional Korean martial arts.

In 1955, the Korean dojangs were unified. A Korean general named Choi Hong Hi named the combined Korean

The beach is a peaceful setting for these men to practice tae kwon do maneuvers.

martial arts tae kwon do. This means the "way" *(do)* of punching, or striking, with the "hand" *(tae)* and "foot" *(kwon)*. The name recalled the traditional teachings of tae kwon, again demonstrating the national pride that was so important to Korea as a newly freed country.

Since 1955, tae kwon do has developed very quickly. It was first demonstrated at the Olympics in 1988, and it became an Olympic sport in 2000. It is now the most popular martial art in the world.

FORMS, SPARRING, AND BREAKING BOARDS

LEARNING TAE KWON DO IS NOT EASY. IT

takes years of training to strengthen both the mind and body of

the student. But it can be a lot of fun!

Proper manners, including respect for the opponent, are important in tae kwon do.

Kicking technique is perfected by practicing against a target.

Breaking is the third part of tae kwon do training, after forms and sparring. Students use chops, punches, or kicks to break boards. This teaches focus and concentration, and helps to perfect the kicks and blows.

Beginning students use foam training boards that break easily, to learn the proper way to deliver a punch or kick. As they learn more, they move up to wooden boards and then to stacks of boards. Very advanced students can break bricks, tiles, blocks of ice, or even baseball bats!

A display of breaking by a tae kwon do master is very exciting. A master can use all of tae kwon do's dramatic leaps and spins to break boards held at every angle. Boards are even held high in the air by one student sitting on another's shoulders. The master has to leap high in the air to break the board with a soaring, flying spin kick!

A skilled martial artist can break boards dramatically with a kick or a hit.

CHAPTER THREE

THE ART OF PUNCHING AND KICKING

TAE KWON DO IS BEST KNOWN FOR ITS

kicking. A tae kwon do master can call on a wide variety of kicking techniques. In competition, only kicks, not hand strikes, are allowed to the head.

Historical reasons might explain the importance of kicking in tae kwon do. Originally, tae kwon do was mostly a military art. The Hwarangdo knights used their martial arts

Tae kwon do's maneuvers are often practiced alone before sparring with a partner.

training to fight other soldiers. Those soldiers often wore armor or fought on horseback. So a kick to the head might be the only way a Hwarangdo knight could use his martial arts—the rest of the opponent would be protected by armor. Likewise, to reach someone on horseback, you'd better be able to kick pretty high!

Whatever the reasons are for its importance in the early days, there are good reasons that kicking is so important today. It's simple: Your legs are much stronger than your arms. They carry all of your weight around all day, whether you are running, walking, or just standing. Your legs lift your whole body off the ground when you jump. Try that standing on your hands! Most people can't stand on their hands at all, let alone walk, run, or jump. Because your legs are stronger than your arms, a kick can be delivered with much greater force than a punch.

Legs are longer than arms, too. Because the leg reaches out farther than the arm, the kicker can attack from farther away, which is an advantage.

The problem with kicking is that when you have one leg up in the air for a kick, you will not be as balanced as you would be on both feet. In tae kwon do, that stability is often traded for the additional power and reach a kick provides.

But tae kwon do doesn't only teach kicking. Blocking

In competition, opponents are protected by padding and helmets.

techniques and hand strikes are also taught. We'll talk about those first.

The best way to avoid getting hit is to not be there when the blow arrives. Part of learning tae kwon do is learning to **evade** attacks. It is helpful to stay in constant motion so that the opponent is never given a good, steady target.

If you can't evade the attack, one of tae kwon do's blocking techniques will help to stop it. Most blocks are made when the forearm comes down across the opponent's arm or leg to block the kick or punch. This is why pads are worn on the fore-arms in free sparring and competition.

A low block, done by chopping down the forearm, blocks a kick that is coming up. A high block might be used to protect your head from an axe kick coming down from above. Inner blocks come across the blocker's body to stop a strike or a kick coming from the opposite side. Outer blocks come from the center position and swing out to stop attacks coming from the same side as the blocking arm.

Every member of the family can benefit from practicing tae kwon do.

Evasion and blocks allow some defense in a tae kwon do match. However, tae kwon do is mostly an aggressive, offensive art. Punches and—especially—kicks are its bread and butter.

While tae kwon do is best known for its kicking, hand strikes are important, too. After all, the term *tae kwon do* means "the way of kicking and punching." Punches are allowed in tae kwon do competitions if they are delivered to the body. Hand strikes are also important when learning tae kwon do for self-defense. Hand strikes can be delivered more quickly than kicks and with less effect on the striker's balance.

Tae kwon do's hand strikes include not only punches with a closed fist but also a variety of other attacks. Stiffened fingers can be used vertically (a "spear hand") or horizontally (a "knife hand"). This type of attack is most effective on a small area of the body that might not take a blow from the whole fist. Knife and spear hands are used on "soft" targets such as the stomach, where there is no bone close to the surface. A knife hand to the head, where the hard skull is right beneath the skin, would be more likely to injure the attacker's hand than the defender's head.

Strikes with the meaty palm, or heel, of the hand, can be delivered to harder targets. With your hand bent back at the wrist, you can deliver a palm strike with less risk of injury

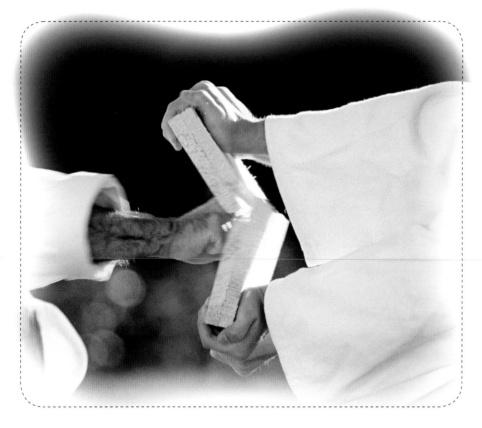

A hand strike is capable of delivering a powerful blow.

to the hand. Other hand strikes are delivered with the outside edge of the hand (chops) or with the inside edge, with the thumb folded in for safety (ridge hands).

Tae kwon do's many exciting kicks are what make it so much fun to watch. Not long ago, tae kwon do's kicking arsenal was limited to just a few kicks. The front snap kick and the roundhouse kick were the main ones. But in the last 20 years or so, a wide variety of kicking techniques has been added. Today, the strategy of a tae kwon do match can be as complicated as a game of chess.

Front kicks can be delivered quickly, shot straight out like a boxer's jab. Roundhouse kicks come sweeping in from the side. They arrive more slowly than front kicks, but they have more force.

The axe kick is just what it sounds like. The kicker's foot is raised high over his head and brought straight down like an

Here's what it would look like if your opponent came at you with a kick!

axe, with great force. Side kicks are delivered straight out to the side, with the blade of the foot backed by all of the body's weight. Back kicks are similar to front kicks, only in reverse. The kicker shoots his heel straight back, like a mule, surprising an attacker coming up from behind. In a hook kick, the kicker lifts the leg high, then snaps the lower half of it across like a whip, bringing the kick in from a surprising and effective angle.

Beginners are first taught to kick low. They practice delivering the kicks to low targets so that they can develop proper technique without losing their balance. As they gain experience, they lift the kicks higher and higher. This early practice helps them with their balance later, even when kicking with their feet higher than their heads!

At this point, students learn to add spins and leaps to their kicks. No matter how big you are, it's not easy to defend yourself against a flying side kick! These spinning and leaping kicking techniques are probably tae kwon do's best-known feature. Their exciting nature makes tae kwon do a fun sport to watch and learn.

The experienced tae kwon do student can choose from a wide variety of offensive and defensive moves. Part of the strategy of any match is to choose the right punching, kicking, blocking, and evasion techniques in different situations.

CHAPTER FOUR

ETIQUETTE, RESPECT, AND SELF-CONTROL

LEARNING TAE KWON DO MEANS LEARNING

more than just a better way to fight. You also learn behaviors and values that can improve all aspects of your life. These basic points, or principles, remain the backbone of instruction in most dojangs today. Students are taught to honor their country, their family, and their flag. They are taught to be brave, honest, and upright.

Perseverance—the willingness and ability to stick to a task—is learned through the hard physical training of tae kwon do. Integrity—doing things the right way—is taught through strictly following and learning the techniques and poom say. Cooperation is learned through training as a group. For

WON KWANG'S FIVE PRINCIPLES

Because tae kwon do began as a military art, some of the strict military code lies at the base of its teachings. The Hwarangdo knights followed the philosophy of an ancient priest named Won Kwang Bopsa. Won Kwang's teachings focused on five important principles:

1. Have loyalty to your king or country.
2. Have respect for your parents.
3. Be honorable and honest to your friends.
4. Never retreat in battle.
5. Do not take a life without cause.

These kids get a kick out of their tae kwon do practice!

example, in step sparring, if the students do not cooperate in executing the proper techniques, someone is likely to get hurt. Etiquette, or good manners, is learned through the formalized bowing and other dojang rules of behavior.

Finally, as with most martial arts, tae kwon do can do wonders for your self-control and self-confidence. Discipline and self-control are stressed in all dojangs. In fact, they are necessary to complete the training. And as you develop your skills, your confidence in yourself cannot help but get stronger.

SELF-DEFENSE

PEOPLE STUDY TAE KWON DO FOR

training, for exercise, and to improve their lives. But tae kwon do is also taught for self-defense. Its teachings always begin with the idea that physical conflicts should be avoided if at all possible. However, tae kwon do students learn important and effective self-defense lessons in case of attack.

Tae kwon do is a great way to improve your physical health and mental awareness.

This girl may be little, but she delivers a big kick!

Obviously, the hand strikes, kicks, blocks, and evasion techniques described earlier are useful in self-defense. But self-defense training begins before you are ever in a position to throw a punch.

The most important self-defense lesson is how to avoid being a target. You need to pay attention to your surroundings and not get into a dangerous situation. If someone appears threatening, or if an area is dark or empty, you avoid it. In addition, it is helpful to stand or walk with dominant, confident body language. People slumping their shoulders or averting their eyes might be seen as easier targets.

One of the many benefits of tae kwon do is learning self-defense.

If a fight cannot be avoided, advanced tae kwon do training includes self-defense techniques. These are too dangerous to use in sparring competitions. For example, force can be applied to certain places on the body, known as pressure points, to cause pain and control an attacker. With proper technique and only a little pressure, even by one hand, an expert can drop the biggest opponent to the ground. Pressure-point techniques can be used to cause pain (the *tong hyel* technique), paralysis (*ma hyel*), or even death (*sa hyel*). These techniques are taught to only the most advanced masters and are used only in the most extreme situations.

Of course, the vast majority of students never use any of these techniques. Most students also never use their art in any real-life self-defense situations. For most people, tae kwon do is a great way to exercise and to learn the behaviors and values that open up possibilities in all areas of life.

GLOSSARY

arsenal—a place where weapons are kept; also, a person's collection of weapons or powers

dojang—a tae kwon do school

dynasty—a period of time during which one person or one family rules a region

evade—to escape or try to get away from

sparring—the activity of practice fighting

tranquil—calm, peaceful

TIMELINE

2300 B.C.   The legendary King Tangun ("the holy warrior") founds the land that will later become Korea.

1100 B.C.   The first of the Korea Peninsula's three kingdoms, Koguryo, is created. The smallest kingdom, Silla, develops an elite corps of warriors known as Hwarangdo, who practice a form of martial arts that becomes the basis for modern tae kwon do.

A.D. 1392–1910   In peacetime under the Yi dynasty, martial arts are considered less important, and interest in them starts to die out.

1910   The Japanese conquer Korea and ban the practice of martial arts.

1943   Okinawan karate and Japanese judo are introduced to Korea.

1945   Korea is freed from Japanese rule. The people's newfound spirit of independence leads them to look to traditional Korean fighting styles. Tae kwon and soo bakh begin to be taught, incorporating lessons of karate and kung fu.

1952   Korean president Syng-man Rhee orders all Korean military forces to study tae kwon and soo bakh.

1955   At a conference of Korean martial arts masters, the combined arts are renamed *tae kwon do* ("the way of kicking and punching") by General Choi Hong Hi.

1966   General Choi Hong Hi founds the International Taekwon-Do Federation.

1967   The U.S. Taekwon-Do Association is founded.

1972   The Kukiwon, the world tae kwon do headquarters, is built in Korea.

1988   Tae kwon do debuts as a demonstration sport at the Olympics.

2000   Tae kwon do becomes an official medal sport at the Summer Olympics.

FIND OUT MORE

Books

Charbonnet, Gabrielle. *Princess of Power.* New York: Disney Press, 1999.

Morris, Neil. *Tae Kwon Do.* Chicago: Heinemann Library, 2001.

Perez, Herb. *The Complete Tae Kwon Do Book for Kids.* New York: McGraw-Hill/Contemporary, 1999.

Pinkney, J. Brian. *JoJo's Flying Side Kick.* New York: Simon & Schuster Books for Young Readers, 1995.

Yates, Keith D., and Bryan Robbins. *Tae Kwon Do for Kids.* New York: Sterling, 1998.

On the Web

Visit our home page for lots of links about tae kwon do:
http://www.childsworld.com/links.html

NOTE TO PARENTS, TEACHERS, AND LIBRARIANS: We routinely check our Web links to make sure they're safe, active sites—so encourage your readers to check them out!

INDEX

ABOUT THE AUTHOR

Thomas Buckley is an attorney and writer in Raleigh, North Carolina, who has won several screenwriting awards. In 1997, he was honored to earn a student black belt in Kenpo Karate from Grandmaster Rick Allemany in San Francisco. He has also participated in seminar training in the arts of jujitsu, *arnis, escrima, wing chun,* and kung fu Sansoo. His one-year-old son already has a pretty good front kick and an impressive *ki-ai*, and his five-year-old daughter is formidable!

W.L. Mackenzie King

J.L. Granatstein

Fitzhenry & Whiteside

Contents

THE CANADIANS
A Continuing Series

W.L. Mackenzie King

Author: J.L. Granatstein
Design: Kerry Designs
Cover Illustration: John Mardon

Fitzhenry & Whiteside acknowledge with thanks the support of the Government of Canada through its Book Publishing Industry Development Program, and the Ontario Arts council for their support in our publishing program.

Canadian Cataloguing in Publication Data
Granatstein, J.L., 1939-
(The Canadians) Rev. ed.
Includes bibliographic references and index.
ISBN 1-55041-489-5
1. King, William Lyon Mackenzie, 1874-1950. 2. Prime ministers - Canada - Biography. 3. Canada - Politics and government - 20th century. I. Title. II. Series.

| FC581.K5G73 2002 | 971.062'2'092 | C00-930540-8 |
| | F1033.K53G735 2002 | |

© 2002 Fitzhenry & Whiteside Limited
195 Allstate Parkway, Markham, Ontario L3R 4T8

Prologue

After all the preliminaries were completed, after the stirring orators had roused the crowd in both French and English, the prime minister finally left his seat on the platform and came to the microphone. The Montreal arena fell silent as he began by paying the ritual tributes to the leaders with whom he had shared the platform. Then Mackenzie King got to the meat of his speech:

King with Laurier,
disciple and teacher

It is just thirty-six years ago today that I was invited by Sir Wilfrid Laurier to become a member of his Cabinet...I have had, in the office of prime minister, to go through most of the experiences and many of the trials which Sir Wilfrid encountered in the years he was in office. I am proud indeed to say that...I never failed him once...

I saw Sir Wilfrid defeated by an unholy alliance between the Nationalists of this province and the Tories of the other provinces of Canada. I saw all that grew out of that ignoble and treacherous plot. I need not give you the record. It will be for all time a blot of shame on the pages of our country's history.

But the question I wish to put to you...is whether you, the people of the province of Quebec, intend to allow the tactics of 1911 to be repeated successfully in 1945, and to have Mackenzie King in 1945 suffer the fate of Sir Wilfrid Laurier in 1911?

Just an ordinary campaign speech, this election address of June 2, 1945. King made dozens of them in that election, thousands in the course of his career that lasted thirty years at the head of the Liberal party.

But that speech, however ordinary, is nonetheless very revealing of the man. In the first line, Mackenzie King's obsession with dates and anniversaries leaps out. Who else would have remembered that it had been thirty-six years since he entered the cabinet? Then the link with Sir Wilfrid Laurier, the great French-Canadian prime minister, the greatest Canadian of them all. The speech was designed to remind Quebec that King had been loyal to Laurier, a direct reference to the great conscription crisis of 1917 that had seen Laurier deserted by almost all his English-speaking supporters—except Mackenzie King. King was the heir of Laurier, the inheritor of his tradition of linking French and English Canadians, the recipient of the support of his people. In 1911, Mackenzie King reminded his listeners, the federal Conservatives and the Quebec Nationalists who opposed Laurier's moderation had struck a deal that forced the great leader from power. Now in 1945, King was suggesting, the same type of alliance was in the works. Would Quebec do to King what it had done to Laurier? The roared "non" from thousands of people was the answer Mackenzie King sought.

An ordinary speech, yes. But in it a consummate politician demonstrated just how he kept power. All the carefully designed trigger words were there—Laurier, loyalty, unholy alliance—and all were fully appreciated and believed both by the man who spoke them and by those who listened.

That shared understanding between the man on the platform and the audience, between leader and followers, is the key to political success. And no politician in Canadian history ever had the success of Mackenzie King, a man who held power as prime minister longer than any other man. There are lessons in his political leadership, and this is Mackenzie King's story.

Chapter 1
The Road to Power

The ragged band of rebels marched down Yonge Street toward the centre of York, the heart of the ruling Family Compact's power and strength. At their head came William Lyon Mackenzie, the fiery Scot, the newspaper editor and the former mayor of Toronto. It was 1837; and they were engaged in a fight for

PROCLAMATION.

BY His Excellency SIR FRANCIS BOND HEAD, Baronet, Lieutenant Governor of Upper Canada, &c. &c.

To the Queen's Faithful Subjects in Upper Canada.

In a time of profound peace, while every one was quietly following his occupations, feeling secure under the protection of our Laws, a band of Rebels, instigated by a few malignant and disloyal men, has had the wickedness and audacity to assemble with Arms, and to attack and Murder the Queen's Subjects on the Highway—to Burn and Destroy their Property—to Rob the Public Mails—and to threaten to Plunder the Banks—and to Fire the City of Toronto.

Brave and Loyal People of Upper Canada, we have been long suffering from the acts and endeavours of concealed Traitors, but this is the first time that Rebellion has dared to shew itself openly in the land, in the absence of invasion by any Foreign Enemy.

Let every man do his duty now, and it will be the last time that we or our children shall see our lives or properties endangered, or the Authority of our Gracious Queen insulted by such treacherous and ungrateful men. MILITIA-MEN OF UPPER CANADA, no Country has ever shewn a finer example of Loyalty and Spirit then YOU have given upon this sudden call of Duty. Young and old of all ranks, are flocking to the Standard of their Country. What has taken place will enable our Queen to know Her Friends from Her Enemies—a public enemy is never so dangerous as a concealed Traitor—and now my friends let us complete well what is begun—let us not return to our rest till Treason and Traitors are revealed to the light of day, and rendered harmless throughout the land.

Be vigilant, patient and active—leave punishment to the Laws—our first object is, to arrest and secure all those who have been guilty of Rebellion, Murder and Robbery.—And to aid us in this, a Reward is hereby offered of

One Thousand Pounds,

to any one who will apprehend, and deliver up to Justice, WILLIAM LYON MACKENZIE; and FIVE HUNDRED POUNDS to any one who will apprehend, and deliver up to Justice, DAVID GIBSON—or SAMUEL LOUNT—or JESSE LLOYD—or SILAS FLETCHER—and the same reward and a free pardon will be given to any of their accomplices who will render this public service, except he or they shall have committed, in his own person, the crime of Murder or Arson.

And all, but the Leaders above-named, who have been seduced to join in this unnatural Rebellion, are hereby called to return to their duty to their Sovereign—to obey the Laws—and to live henceforward as good and faithful Subjects—and they will find the Government of their Queen as indulgent as it is just.

GOD SAVE THE QUEEN.

Thursday, 3 o'clock, P. M.
7th Dec.

☞ The Party of Rebels, under their Chief Leaders, is wholly dispersed, and flying before the Loyal Militia. The only thing that remains to be done, is to find them, and arrest them.

R. STANTON, Printer to the QUEEN'S Most Excellent Majesty.

The passing of time sometimes changes and even reverses the reputation that historical figures have had during their lifetimes. Mackenzie King took delight in the contrast between two proclamations hanging on his wall: his own Order of Merit, presented to him by George VI, and this one indicating the opinion of his grandfather held by Queen Victoria's representative in Canada. Today William Lyon Mackenzie is generally regarded as a courageous, if hot-headed, reformer whose life was dedicated to improving the conditions of Upper Canadian society.

After her death, King revered this portrait of his mother. In his diary, he wrote that he could communicate with her spirit and those of others in "the world beyond" through mediums, including his dog, Pat.

freedom and the rights of man, a battle against tyranny and injustice.

This was the stuff on which Mackenzie King was raised. His mother, Isabel, was the daughter of William Lyon Mackenzie and had herself been born in the United States during Mackenzie's exile from Upper Canada after the failure of the rebellion in 1837. To Isabel, to her husband John King, and to their son, William Lyon Mackenzie King, the restoration of the Mackenzie reputation and the vindication of the cause of the rebel of '37 were matters of vital importance.

Mackenzie King was born in Berlin (later Kitchener), Ontario, on December 17, 1874, just thirty-seven years after the rebellion. Everyone over the age of forty-five remembered the ill-fated revolt; thousands had known Mackenzie and the other leaders, and the heirs of the Family Compact, the victors, still held power. Confederation was just seven years old, and the new Dominion seemed already to be as corrupt and ill-governed as ever the colony of Upper Canada had been. In such circumstances, the past was alive for Mackenzie King and his family, and young Willie was never allowed to forget it. Nor did he wish to.

The influence of his mother was enormously powerful. Isabel King was an attractive, strong-willed woman who put all her hopes for the family name on young Willie. He was the favourite son, the second of the family's four children, and she doted on the boy. This affection was returned in full measure, and Mackenzie King in fact remained

King as a small boy

tied to his mother for the rest of his life. The per-fection of Isabel King would always be such as to prevent her son from finding the "right" woman to marry.

By contrast, the role of John King was less forceful. Affection and regard existed between father and son, and his father had a successful law career in Berlin and later in Toronto (at least until fortune turned against the family in the mid-1890s). But there could be little doubt that his mother remained the dominant figure both in the household and in the life of Mackenzie King.

Nor could there be any doubt, given the interests of his mother, that Mackenzie King would turn toward a life of public service. What the precise direction would be was unclear, but his mission in life was not. Young William would work to complete the task of reform started by William Lyon Mackenzie. Perhaps this might

King on his seventeenth birthday, 1891

King (standing) with friends at Harvard

The Road to Power

Clothing factory, London Ontario

lead to the church—when he was nineteen King thought the ministry might be his calling. Perhaps it would lie in the law—and King attended law school and secured his degree although he would never practise.

Perhaps it would come in more prosaic ways. While he was attending the University of Toronto in the 1890s, King began taking an interest in the conditions of life around him. Toronto was not yet a huge city, but it had more than its share of slums, of disease, of young women driven to prostitution by economic need. As a typical young man of his comfortably middle-class upbringing, King ached to help these people. Once a week he would go off to read to patients at the Hospital for Sick Children. He would seek out prostitutes and attempt to persuade them to abandon their trade and turn to God. He was an earnest young man, probably a prig, but he was no fool. He could see the conditions of life in which the majority of people lived, and he knew that those conditions had to improve.

Mackenzie King was also an able student and after his Toronto degrees were completed, he went off to Chicago for graduate work. While there, he worked with the famous Jane Addams at Hull House, the settlement house that tried to meet the needs of Chicago's thousands of immigrants. Later, he went to Harvard where he did a doctoral degree in economics.

At least as important as his formal academic work was young King's study of sweatshop conditions in the Toronto garment industry. In a series of well-researched articles published in the Toronto *Mail and Empire* in the fall of 1897, King put some of his idealism to practical use. Conditions were terrible, and by forcing them to the attention of the public, the way was opened for reform. Indeed, the way opened wide for Mackenzie King. A friend of his father's was the postmaster general in the government of Sir Wilfrid Laurier. William Mulock talked with King about the sweatshop conditions and commissioned the 23-year-old student to prepare a more detailed study.

Mr. Mulock was very kind [King wrote in his diary], *he urged upon me to think more of making provision for myself. He is anxious to effect reform...I make a definite stand on the side of labour, as it involves showing up of corrupt'n and robbery by wealthy men. I will have only the truth no matter what the cost...This has been a happy day and some good accomplished.*

A Toronto sweatshop at the turn of the century

Thus was King's career launched and he had found his first patron.

His report for Mulock was a good one, and some reforms were implemented as a result. More important for King, the postmaster general never forgot the young man with the reforming zeal and the capacity for hard work. In June, 1900, while King was in Rome in the midst of a European stay, Mulock wired him with the offer of a position as editor of the *Labour Gazette*, a new journal the government was starting up. After some hesitation, King accepted and returned to Ottawa, ready to take up his career as a civil servant. Indeed, within days of his return home, King was made deputy minister of the brand-new and tiny department of labour. For a young man, not yet twenty-six, this was starting at the top.

The new posts offered great opportunity, much in line with King's interests. The era of industrialization was upon Canada, and

King in the 1908 campaign

in the boom years of the turn of the century, change was rapid. To many, any change was frightening, particularly if it meant that labour was becoming organized and beginning to demand a greater share for its toil. To others, the problem was that business had grown too big, too powerful, and that competition had been replaced by monopolies and combines that controlled supply and kept prices up. In this jungle, the role of small government was necessarily cautious. But for a young man with ideals and aims, there was still room to manoeuvre.

Certainly King was good at this. For the next eight years he worked in the department of labour, investigating strikes, drafting legislation, handling the increasing work of a growing department. He was an expert in the area at a time when there were very few men in Canada who were. And as he worked in Ottawa, King began to realize the difficulties that faced governments, however good their intentions. Reform was difficult to achieve, and the problems that had seemed so simple to resolve when he was a student now had unheard-of complications. Black and white tended to shade into greys, and caution was a good watchword for a civil servant. Powerful interests had to be approached carefully, government ministers handled with care. The new Jerusalem would not, could not, come overnight. Early on, Mackenzie King came to the realization that in Canada the system would have to be altered gradually or else the reaction to change could be such as to set back the cause forever. He had made himself ready for the next step up the ladder.

Politics was where power lay, King believed. In politics much could be accomplished, and if one were prime minister, there seemed no limits on the good one could achieve. To reach this goal one had first to enter Parliament, serve a political apprenticeship, and join the cabinet. This meant abandoning the civil service and its security for the more uncertain life of electoral politics—no small matter for the none-too-rich Mackenzie King.

Sir Wilfrid Laurier had long been aware of the deputy minister of labour, and from 1905 at least had been looking on him as a potential Liberal candidate and possible cabinet minister. In the general election of 1908, after Laurier had agreed to make the labour department

King with his parents in 1911

stronger and had made vague promises that King might expect to be its minister, the young man made his decision. King announced his candidacy in North Waterloo, Ontario, a constituency that included his home town of Berlin. The result was all King could have hoped; he was victorious, winning the seat against the Conservatives. A few months later, he joined the cabinet as minister of labour. His future seemed assured.

When Laurier introduced the new minister to the House of Commons, his parents watched from the gallery. King was in ecstasy throughout the day, and he reflected on what his success meant for his mother:

...there is reward in this for her as well as me, reward for the sacrifices her father made, and for what she has had to make in consequence. If her father could only have been present too, I would have asked for nothing more. He would have felt a recompense for all his struggle. His life, his work are all kept alive in this way, and that I feel to be my chiefest part.

Laurier at a rally in the 1911 campaign

King still remembered his roots, his goals. He would never forget them.

The new minister's tasks were not entirely dissimilar to those he had handled so well while he was deputy minister. There were the same efforts to resolve strikes, to bring labour and management to the bargaining table, the same attempts to keep public opinion under control. But there were a host of political chores now too: speeches to be made to the House of Commons, royal commissions to be supervised, the general and heavy work of a cabinet minister, and a host of political chores on organizational and publicity matters.

All these tasks were made heavier by the growing weaknesses of the Laurier government. The Liberals had been in power since 1896, and no government after fifteen years of office is quite so skillful and sensitive at responding to crises as it was at the beginning. Ministers tend to think they can do no wrong, that they know best, and the party organization inevitably begins to fall apart. Laurier's regime suffered from advanced old age, and in 1911 when the government tried to bring in a measure advocating reciprocity in trade with the United States, Liberalism went down to defeat at the polls. Free trade with the Americans threatened to upset old and established trading patterns, and this change worried businesspeople, manufacturers, and even many farmers who feared that it meant Canada might soon be swallowed whole by its giant neighbour to the south.

For Mackenzie King, after just two years in the cabinet, the defeat of the government came as a shattering blow. Worse, Waterloo North fell to the Conservatives. Mackenzie King was out of Parliament and out of work.

For the next three years he lived by doing odd jobs, writing for the press, making speeches, doing political chores for the Liberal party. Not until 1914 did his life take on a more structured pattern. In the summer of that year he was asked to work as an expert in labour relations for the Rockefeller Foundation. John D. Rockefeller had founded Standard Oil, one of the world's giant corporations, and his wealth was so huge that a substantial portion of it was invested in the Foundation. Now Mackenzie King would study labour problems and, more directly, help the Rockefeller interests resolve a long and bitter strike in the coal fields of Colorado. Again King had found a valued patron.

John D. Rockefeller. Rockefeller's descendants have become an American dynasty.

The labour expert spent most of the next several years working for the Rockefellers. His role in resolving the Colorado conflict was controversial and many later observers believed that King betrayed his principles by helping to create a company union there. But to King, his goals remained crystal clear: the need was to ensure industrial peace and to help humanize the relationships of the capital and labour. And certainly none would doubt that conditions in the Colorado mines were better after King had finished his work than they were before.

Indeed, King's Colorado experience had led him seriously to consider the whole problem of the role of industry in the modern state. How could industry produce the goods efficiently yet not crush the spirits and bodies of the people at the same time? How could industry operate in a humane fashion? *Industry and Humanity*, his book published in 1918, was the result of all his study and thought on the subject.

The book is almost unreadable, written in muddy prose and full

Robert Borden

of soppy moralism. But it was an important work in its day, the first statement by a Canadian of the need to create industrial democracy. King's experiences in resolving strikes had shaped his understanding of the nature of society, and he knew the terrible effects that strikes could have on communities. The answer lay in his Colorado scheme, he believed; it lay in creating and fostering love and understanding, trust and regard, a true Christianity on the part of management and labour. All this could be expressed through a scheme of corporate welfare, designed to help the workers, through grievance procedures, employee bills of rights and the like. The book was King's summation of his experiences, his accounting of his life and what he had learned from his first sweatshop investigations in 1897 through to the Colorado mines.

Because of his work for the Rockefeller Foundation, King was out of Canada for much of the period after 1914. The Great War had begun in August, 1914, and soon Canada became involved to the hilt. Men were recruited in huge numbers; industry became harnessed to the war effort, and farmers mobilized to produce the food needed to support the vast armies in Europe. Canada had been unprepared for war, and soon the demands of the struggle began to tear the country apart.

The key question was conscription. Should the government have the power to compel men to join the army? By 1917, the Conservative government under Sir Robert Borden had decided that the needs of the war required this step. For Laurier, still leading the Liberal party, this was a terrible question. As a French Canadian, he knew all too well that Quebec remained deeply opposed to conscription for service in what his compatriots saw as a British war. As a Canadian, he knew that English Canadians were by and large equally determined that every fit man should go. And soon Laurier saw his party begin to split, with the English-speaking Liberals deserting him to join Borden's coalition, the Union government. Conscription had forced the country into two camps, French- and English-speaking.

What of Mackenzie King? He knew that conscription was a divisive issue, and he feared that unless it were implemented with the cooperation of both the major peoples of Canada it would wreck the country. Could Laurier not agree to it? No, he could not. The choice then fell upon King: would he stay with Laurier and the Liberals or would he go with the Union government? After some hesitation, King made the fateful decision—he would remain a Laurier Liberal.

In the election of December, 1917, Mackenzie King, like most Liberals in English Canada, suffered defeat at the polls. The Union government was returned to power with a substantial majority, and Laurier had only a solid Quebec behind him. The split had occurred, and although conscription would be enforced, it would produce relatively few reinforcements for the bloodbath in France and Flanders; it would, however, produce lasting grievances in Quebec and deep resentment in English Canada.

For Mackenzie King, however, the 1917 election was a turning point. In his eyes, and in the eyes of many others, he had become the heir of Laurier, the next leader of the Liberal party. Had he not stood loyally beside the Old Chief when all others were deserting him? Did he not deserve his reward?

In 1919, after an exhausted Laurier had died, King went to the Liberal party's leadership convention, the first open convention ever held in Canada. He intended to win, and his strengths were many. By 1919 the war was over, and the bloodshed at the front had been replaced by industrial warfare at home. In Winnipeg, for example, a great general strike had paralyzed the city and blood had been spilled. Radicals seemed to be everywhere, organizing and plotting. People were afraid.

Who better to calm their fears than an expert on labour relations, a scholar who had written a book? Who better to select as leader than a still-young man of forty-five who had served his political apprenticeship under Laurier? Who better than a Laurier loyalist who was from Ontario and who might help the Liberals break out of Quebec? And when Mackenzie King made a great speech at the convention, many uncommitted delegates decided that he was the man of the hour. Quebec's delegates backed him solidly, he had good support in Ontario, and on the fourth ballot he won.

Mackenzie King had become leader of the Liberal party.

Chapter 2
Prime Minister

The new Liberal leader was something of an unknown quantity to the country. Those who followed politics closely remembered him as minister of labour; those who had been wrapped up in the politics and patriotism of the war years regarded him with some suspicion, as one who had worked for much of the war in the United States and as one who had been "soft" on conscription. He was seen as a bright young man—to be only forty-five in politics in 1919 was still to be young—and as a mildly progressive expert on labour questions. But could this man be prime minister of Canada? No one knew this yet.

Only Mackenzie King had no doubts. He was the leader of the Liberal party, a man with confidence in his own abilities and in his pre-ordained destiny to be leader of the nation. King's confidence was not unjustified. He could do enormous amounts of work and had always been able to get results. The work in the United States for the Rockefellers had convinced him of his mediating powers in difficult situations—and of his ability to get along with the rich and powerful. King had been in the cabinet under Laurier, and he knew that these traits were essential for a Canadian prime minister. He was as well travelled as any Canadian political leader before him; he knew England and the United States, two nations of obvious importance to Canada, and he was on friendly terms with many of the leading figures in the two great English-speaking powers. And then there was his education. No Canadian leader before King had as much formal education, including a doctorate in economics. The qualifications seemed formidable, but Mackenzie King himself was well aware of his liabilities too.

First, the Liberal leader was a bachelor. This was not a crushing drawback, but a wife would have been a help in carrying out the social obligations that fall on a public man. More important still, King was a man with a great many acquaintances but few close friends. A wife would have been a partner with whom confidences could be shared, someone with whom the lonely King could have found companionship. Instead King had his dogs, deeply loved, and his diary, an extraordinary document into which he poured his soul

King in 1920

Prime Minister

and his secrets. His mother had been his inspiration, but she was gone now, leaving a void that could never be filled. He would be lonely to the end of his days.

But he would be busy. His hours would always be filled with political meetings and conferences with financial backers and important local or regional politicians. He would work hard and he would expect those who served him to match his pace. Secretaries were expected to be on call at any hour, and powerful figures in Ottawa became weary from answering King's late-night telephone calls with their impossible demands. He was fussy, a perfectionist, a man who sometimes believed that the only way to get a job done well was to do it himself. No one who worked for King liked him; all those who did, admired his capacity, his judgment, and his finely tuned political skills. He would need all these traits to meet the challenges he faced in 1919.

His first task had to be the reconstruction of his party. The war had shattered the Liberals, dividing French from English and wrecking the party's organization in the west and in Ontario. Now everyone had to be encouraged to return to the party. A light would be placed in the window, and all who had sinned could return home. This had to be done in such a fashion that the loyalist Liberals and the French-speaking Québécois in particular did not feel betrayed—no easy task.

In addition, there was the problem of the farmers. After years as the poor relations of Confederation, farmers by the end of the war had had enough and had organized their own political party, the Progressives. Many of the farmers were traditional Liberals, including much of the leadership, and King had to manoeuvre so that the Liberal party again would be the logical place for all to return to when, as he expected would be inevitable, politics got back to normal.

But when would "normal" begin? The war had upset everything in Canada. Sixty thousand soldiers had died, leaving widows, children and disillusionment behind them. The country continued to be divided over conscription. The cost of living had skyrocketed and wages had not kept pace, creating great unrest among labour. And the government of Sir Robert Borden, still nominally a Union government of Conservatives and Liberals, was beginning to break up. Indeed, Borden himself was tired, made old before his time by the strains of the war. And in 1920 he would step down, turning over command to Arthur Meighen, an able man but one who had had to do all the difficult chores for the government during and after the war and one who, as a result, had made enemies across the length and breadth of the land.

Meighen was a vigorous leader, a forthright man of honesty and purpose. His task had to be the restoration of a strong government and he turned to this with a will. The place to begin in his view was with tariff policy, the question of determining the rates the government should fix on goods imported into Canada. Tariffs had always been the basis of Canada's National Policy, and a high tariff had been traditional Conservative policy from Sir John A. Macdonald's day. Meighen believed in a tariff high enough to encourage Canadian manufacturers and to provide jobs to workers. His view was clear, possibly even correct, but all Progressives rejected it. Meighen was also forthright about his war record. "I favoured conscription," he told an audience in Quebec. "I introduced the Military Service Act [of 1917]... because I thought it was right." That was magnificent, politics as it should be. But not politics as it is.

Much safer, much sounder was Mackenzie King's careful tactic of saying very little at great length, of talking enthusiastically about the tariff in Ontario, and sounding lukewarm in the west. Policy matters

Conservative leader Arthur Meighen. Meighen concentrated heavily on the tariff as his main issue in the election of 1921 and was rejected by the voters.

were too complex to be settled in an election, King believed. Much better, therefore, to focus on the grievances that existed everywhere, to point to Meighen's sometimes autocratic style, to remind Quebec of the indignities the province had suffered during the war. This was leadership of a kind, but very different from Meighen's method of confronting issues and educating the public. And it was not at all like that of William Lyon Mackenzie.

What it was, however, was successful. In the election of 1921, Mackenzie King's Liberals won a narrow victory, capturing 116 of 235 seats in the House of Commons. The Meighen government was destroyed, a casualty of the war, falling to a mere 50 seats. And the Progressives held 64 seats and more than 20 per cent of the popular vote. The tactic of saying little had worked. But the new prime minister still had no majority in Parliament, and the divisions in the country were terribly evident. This would be no time for strong leadership; this would be the hour for the man of caution, the balancer and juggler. Success in the long term would go to the man who could unite the country and rebuild the party.

Probably this would have been King's style whatever the political makeup of the House of Commons. He had his long-range priorities—what politician, what individual doesn't? But he was shrewd enough to know that politics is a pragmatic business, that various interests have to be satisfied, that no one can forge ahead faster than public opinion will permit. Mackenzie King had learned this as a civil servant and as a minister in Laurier's government. Now he would make it an iron law of Canadian politics.

For four years between 1921 and 1925, the King government did its task with some competence but without style. The prime minister demonstrated that he was a cautious, rather grey personality who showed little flair in meeting the public. Nor were there any initiatives in policy areas to startle anyone. He juggled the tariff in minor ways; he tinkered with railway rates and made them more favourable to prairie farmers; he effectively disbanded the armed forces; and his government's policy within the British Empire was cautiously nationalistic. There seemed to be no change.

Except that change existed not far beneath the surface. In its bland way, King's government had begun the task of binding up the wounds of the nation. Quebec was being re-integrated and gradually the war was being forgotten. The Progressives, torn apart by dissension on the best way to proceed in Parliament, were starting to collapse as a party and the Liberals began to pick up the pieces. The prosperity of the 1920s tended to diminish the labour unrest that had seemed a permanent fact of life at the end of the war in 1918 and 1919. Matters were getting back to normal.

A confident Prime Minister King, therefore, went to the people in 1925. It was the time for a Liberal majority government, King said. It was time to increase immigration, to reform the Senate, to establish a commonsense tariff. It was, clearly, time for more of the same, for more grey, competent government. But the voters did not seem impressed, and the election results saw Meighen lead the Conservatives to 116 seats while the Progressives fell to only 24. King's Liberals had 99. "Expectations have not been realized," a gloomy prime minister wrote in his diary. But "the times will continue to improve...and we may get thro' a session in which event we will be able to carry on—I have 'faith and courage'..."

Incredibly, King refused to concede defeat. Meighen and the Tories had won the election, or at least had won more seats than King. But Meighen himself remained well short of a majority, and

King banked on his ability to win the support of the remaining
Progressives and thus hold onto power. It was daring politics, an
indication that when pressed, King would fight with cleverness to
retain control.

He would need all his wits. To keep the support of crucial independent members of Parliament, King and his cabinet conceded the
necessity for old age pensions early in 1926. Rather, King used the
necessity to win the votes of left-labour members in the House to
pressure his colleagues to concede that the ideal time had come. He

himself had always supported the idea of old age pensions, but the time had never been opportune before. Now it was.

More difficult to control was an unfolding scandal in the department of customs and excise. Civil servants, it soon became clear, had connived in the smuggling of liquor into the United States, in the smuggling of automobiles into Canada, and in widespread corruption and slackness. Even a cabinet minister had dirtied his hands in the affair, and it seemed that the administration of justice had been corrupted, too. The customs scandal would have been a serious crisis in the best of circumstances; in the delicate political balancing act of 1926 it could spell disaster for the Liberals. Before too long it seemed evident that the House of Commons would vote to censure the government, a fatal blow to the Liberal party, and a possible end to the prime minister's political career.

How could this disaster be averted? King thought he had found the way when he went to the governor general, Viscount Byng of Vimy (a wartime general who had commanded the Canadians in France at the time of their great victory at Vimy Ridge in 1917) and asked him to dissolve Parliament. In effect, King wanted a new election, one that would be called before Parliament could pronounce its verdict on the customs scandal. This request was probably unprecedented, but King justified his action by saying to himself and to all who would listen that the public could judge the government just as well as could Parliament. There was only one flaw in this argument—Byng refused to dissolve Parliament as his prime minister wanted.

Governors general in 1926 were already relics of the past, cutters of ribbons, layers of cornerstones. But they still had some real powers, and the power to grant or refuse a dissolution to a prime minister remained. Ordinarily, every governor general did what his prime minister wanted; but these were not ordinary times, or so Byng thought, and he flatly refused to go along.

Mackenzie King was outraged. This British soldier was interfering in the domestic politics of Canada. The prime minister resigned in a huff. Arthur Meighen, the leader of the largest party in Parliament, was called on by Byng, and Meighen agreed to take on the responsibilities of office. The new prime minister set about establishing his administration and carried on in the House of Commons. King's career should have been finished, Meighen's assured.

But here the grandson of the rebel of 1837 had found his issue. Grandfather had fought autocracy; he would, too. Byng's actions destroyed democracy, a charge that seemed to gather force when Meighen was beaten on a vote of confidence in the House of

Commons and when the new prime minister received the dissolution that Byng had refused King. The whole thing smelled, King believed. Byng had acted unconstitutionally in refusing him the dissolution; he had acted unconstitutionally in giving it to Meighen when he had quickly demonstrated his inability to govern. The issue now was the safeguarding of the constitution; the right of Canadians to govern themselves had been thrown into question. An aroused Liberal party stormed to the polls, its corruption forgotten in the smokescreen of debate on the constitutional liberties of the people.

The results seemed predictable: King and his party were returned to power with a comfortable majority. Poor Arthur Meighen, with victory in his grasp, had watched it slip away again. Constitutional arguments had triumphed over charges of corruption.

Or had they? Who knows why people mark their "X" on the ballot? Did the voters understand the subtleties of the questions that King spoke to them about? Did they care about the charges of corruption Meighen made? Some undoubtedly did, but many, many more probably thought that this was just the politicians fighting about nothing again. In the final analysis, elections are probably won by three things: by party organization, by the work of local

King campaigning at Cobourg, Ontario. Note the misspelling of King's name. King, the pragmatist, defeated Meighen, the man of principle.

Hectic activity on the New York Stock Exchange, two days before the collapse of 1929

candidates, and by the way the party leader is perceived. The Liberal organization was not perfect but it worked, and the candidates got out and argued the party case as well as they could.

Most important perhaps was the straight and simple question of Mackenzie King versus Arthur Meighen. The two looked different, sounded different, and led differently. Meighen was direct, straight, blunt; King devious, clever, probably tricky. But King did not divide the country the way Meighen did. He did not bring to memory old hatreds and stress national division as Meighen seemed to do. He

Prime Minister

was cautious and safe; Meighen seemed the reverse. In such a circumstance, perhaps the voters thought it better to go with King. Voters in Quebec made this choice, and so did electors on the prairies, and the results showed Mackenzie King's Liberals with 128 seats and the Conservatives with only 91.

The 1926 election ended Meighen's political career for fifteen years. To be defeated cleanly and fairly was one thing, but to lose to that puffy little man who could never make a simple and straightforward statement about anything was another. Better to get out of politics than go through that again. Meighen resigned as leader of the Conservative party, to be succeeded by a Calgary lawyer and millionaire, Richard Bennett.

And King was back in charge. The times continued good, the economy booming. Canada's population passed the ten million mark, her people wealthier than ever before. It seemed as if the boom of the 1920s would go on forever. And in such good times there seemed little need for a government to engage in experiments.

People seemed to want what King gave them: a small government that did not tinker; a more or less well-run government that helped business exploit and develop the nation; above all, a government that minded its own business and took no radical initiatives in foreign affairs. The best government was the government that governed least. That was one cliché of the period. Another was that the business of government was business. Both of these sayings were true enough in Canada, where no one wanted or expected more.

At least not until the boom went bust. On October 24, 1929, the New York Stock Exchange suffered a catastrophic drop in the prices of shares, and soon the ripples spread across the world. Stocks began to plummet, and shareholders found themselves going broke in a few days. Soon companies closed their doors or cut back, and unemployment began to climb. Wheat sales, a matter of great concern to prairie farmers, began to fall, and rail freight-car movements dropped as a result, throwing thousands more out of work. The country, the world, seemed to be grinding to a halt.

Was Mackenzie King worried? Yes, he was, but this kind of crash happened every few years. There was nothing fundamentally wrong with Canada and people should just be patient. Everything remained for the best in the best of all possible worlds.

But nothing was for the best. Mackenzie King seemed blind to the impact of the Depression. He could not understand its effects on the nation; he could not measure the way being out of work destroyed men and their families; he could not assess accurately the effect of grasshoppers and drought and poor markets on the wheat crop raised by a Saskatchewan farmer. King was not alone in being blind. All

R.B. Bennett would be prime minister from 1930 to 1935, the worst years of the Depression

politicians everywhere reacted in the same way, as did businesspeople, the press, even the public. If people were in difficulties it must be their own fault. Everyone who had been sensible was all right.

But nothing was all right, not even politics. And when the Liberal government went to the public in 1930 with its message that better times were coming, Bennett and the Conservatives trounced the Liberals. The Great Depression would be Bennett's problem for at least five years.

Mackenzie King had not expected to lose this election. But he was a realist and he accepted his loss calmly. "I have gone down if I have with flying colours. A fine record of Government...& before more difficult times come." What did it mean? "It looks as tho' it means Bennett for a while," he wrote in his diary, "then a Liberal party with a long lease of power later on...I believe it is all for the best..."

His prediction was partly accurate. The Liberals would return to power for a long term. But nothing was all for the best, not for a long time to come.

Chapter 3
The Road to War

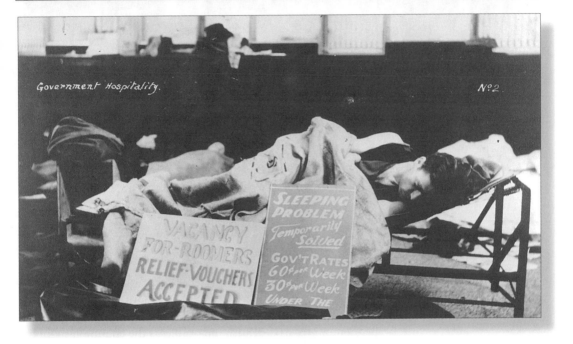

Government Hospitality. N°2.

VACANCY
FOR-ROOMERS
RELIEF-VOUCHERS
ACCEPTED

SLEEPING
PROBLEM
Temporarily
Solved
GOV'T RATES
60¢ per Week
30¢ per Week
Under The

" **C**an you possibly help us," a woman in rural Saskatchewan wrote to Prime Minister Bennett in the midst of the Great Depression, "as we are down and out. My husband is in very poor health & cannot work to keep me & my four children he is a returned man, & sure did his bit in the great war from 1915 until 1919 and absolutely no good now, in fact no man will employ him, because he cannot do a days work for a days pay, & in this town they give no relief...my husband is getting desperate because he knows his wife and kiddies are starving when there is plenty in the land."

That was the Depression in Canada—men, women and children starving when there was the potential of plenty in the land. The system had collapsed, and no one knew how to fix it. Not Prime Minister Bennett. Not Mackenzie King. Not the great captains of

Many unemployed men sought government relief during the Depression

The Road to War

27

King on board the Conte
di Savoia *in November,*
1934

*In his fifth year in power, the
Conservative prime minister,
in desperation, proposed to
Parliament a number of
reforms modelled on those
introduced by President
Roosevelt's government in the
United States. The Judicial
Committee of the Privy
Council, in England, later
ruled that they were unconsti-
tutional.*

industry. No one.

Bennett did try to deal with the problems the country faced. His
government allocated unprecedented sums of money for relief in
1930 and 1931, but the numbers of men without work were also
unprecedented. He first tried to cut government spending, the
remedy urged by most orthodox economists. He later tried to
increase spending, a remedy urged by other theorists. He gave
speeches. He introduced a New Deal in 1935 and proposed some
good legislation. But nothing seemed able to break the grip of
poverty over Canada and its people.

Mackenzie King had the good fortune to be out of power from
1930 to 1935, the worst years of the Depression. To be in office
seemed to be almost a guarantee of defeat in the next election. It
was far easier to oppose the government—after all, that was the
duty of the leader of the Opposition. It was far safer to criticize
than to propose remedies. Mackenzie King could do this, and for
the five years he remained out of office he watched the

The Road to War

King with his 1937 cabinet. Among the more prominent members: 1) C.D. Howe, Ontario; 2) T.A. Crerar, Manitoba; 3) Raoul Dandurand, Quebec; 4) Norman Rogers, Ontario; 5) J.L. Ilsley, Nova Scotia; 6) Ian Mackenzie, British Columbia; 7) J.G. Gardiner, Saskatchewan.

Conservative government grapple with impossible problems and collapse in failure. In the election of 1935, the Liberals were returned to power with a huge majority. The party had campaigned on the slogan "King or Chaos," but what it stood for, what it would do, no one knew. The electors didn't care. All they knew was that King had to be better than Bennett.

Perhaps he would be. But Mackenzie King's solution to the Depression was the same as Bennett's; keep taxes low, reduce spending, encourage trade. Nothing of this sort could work, although conditions seemed to be gradually getting better and unemployment began to ease slightly.

But there were some alterations. Shortly after the election, Mackenzie King created a National Employment Commission to propose changes to the relief system and to suggest ways to create employment. The commission did these things, but it also produced the radical suggestion that Ottawa instead of the provinces should assume the responsibility for the costs of unemployment relief. More radical yet was the idea that the federal government should spend heavily in times of depression. The pump had to be primed before it would work, the commission said, and the federal government was the only source of money.

The Road to War

These ideas tended to worry Mackenzie King. The new and untried always worried the prime minster, by now sixty-one years old and very set in his ways. But gradually the suggestions of the commission lost their strangeness, and by 1938 King had moved a substantial distance toward them. In 1940 his government passed an Unemployment Insurance measure, and deficit financing— deliberately spending more than the government received in taxes—had been tried cautiously a year or so earlier.

But by the time the government had begun experimenting with these methods, everyone's attention was directed away from the long lines outside the downtown soup kitchens. The threat of war had once again been loosed upon the world. Adolph Hitler in Germany, Benito Mussolini in Italy, Emperor Hirohito in Japan and a host of lesser dictators made threatening noises at their neighbours, and the frightening headlines became a regular daily event. The thirties were a different period in every way.

But what did it matter to Canada if Europe went to war? The Dominion was in North America, protected by two great oceans from the madmen of Europe and Asia. The United States was great, powerful and friendly, and no harm could come to Canada so long as it remained so.

Many believed this, and they were not wrong. But Canada was still part of the British Empire, and millions of Canadians assumed that if Britain got involved in a major war Canada would have to do its duty, too. That duty would mean raising hundreds of thou- sands of soldiers, equipping them and shipping them across the ocean to fight the godless enemy, whoever it might be this time. It was all so simple, so terrible.

Nothing worried Mackenzie King more than the thought of war. He knew all too clearly what war would do to Canada. The fiery patriots would demand that troops go to fight for king and country. Other fiery patriots would insist that Canada owed noth- ing to England, that her duty was to deal with unemployment, not to fight in wars that concerned no one in North America. The fighting at home would be terrible, the English-Canadian majority would get its way eventually, and there would be another conscrip- tion crisis, another shattering blow to national unity.

For all his time in office, from 1921 in fact, Mackenzie King had been haunted by these fears. His policy throughout the 1920s had been to create the opportunity for Canada to act in an inde- pendent fashion. He had done this through various legal means at a series of imperial conferences, through appointing diplomats abroad, through a deliberate policy of non-involvement in world affairs. His usual line when action was demanded of Canada was to reply that "Parliament will decide." But Parliament was often out of session, and when it was, it often never got the chance to decide.

King's policy was full of trickery here, of course, but it may have been necessary. The discussion of foreign policy, of war and peace, was not very sophisticated in Canada in the 1920s and 1930s, and the press continued to be all too eager to stir up a crisis, to fan the flames of war. It would be better, King reasoned, to confuse everyone, to delay, in the hopes that the problems might go away.

But if the problems wouldn't disappear, King had no doubt how he would react. Canada was a British nation, and if Great Britain ever became involved again in a major war in a just cause, then Canada would do its part. This was King's own belief, deeply held; it was also a political decision, for every politician in Canada knew that the majority would want this to be so. The important thing had to be to find a way to bring French Canada along willingly with the majority's decision.

And King was convinced that he knew how to do this. The real fear in French Canada was that English Canada would impose conscription, that the government would compel men to serve overseas in a war that Québécois did not and could not see as threatening their safety and interests. How could this threat be eased? To King the answer seemed obvious: Quebec had to be assured that in the event of a European war in which Canada was involved, there would be no conscription for overseas service. Under no circumstances, the prime minister told Parliament on March 30, 1939, would his government do such a thing. His pledge was total, absolute, final and binding on the King government.

Many of King's statements in the 1930s had been deliberately fuzzy and confusing. But not this one about conscription. It was very clear and it had to be. For without this pledge, Quebec would have been at best a reluctant partner in any war, at worst a rebellious province within the state. With it, there might be some cooperation. King had geared everything to the central task as he saw it—to bring a united country into the war, if indeed war became a reality.

Unfortunately the threat of war was very real. The German *Fuehrer*, Adolph Hitler, also had his own plans, and these included swallowing as much of Europe as could be reached. Without war if possible; with war if necessary. From 1933 onward, Germany was the major power on the European continent, and the crises of that decade were German crises: the Rhineland, Austria, the

The Royal Couple leaving Parliament, 1939

Sudetenland, the Polish Corridor. By an extraordinary mixture of bluff, guile and power, Hitler expanded Germany's territory and brought the world to war.

The response of Britain and France, the great European democracies, had been confused and weak. Their people worried over the effects of the Depression, and they seemed not at all eager to go off to fight in another great war. Would Hitler settle for part of what he wanted? Could he be appeased with conces-

The Road to War

sions? At the same time, however, some preparation had to be made, and the British and French defence budgets began to increase, their alliances to be strengthened.

And what of Canada? Could Britain count on the senior Dominion in a time of crisis? The senior British diplomat in Ottawa assured his masters that "it is surely...inconceivable that Canada will not be with us in the end. All I myself really fear is a period of hesitancy..." That was a good judgment in many ways, although it did not take into account Mackenzie King's assessment of the realities that would compel Canada to go to war.

But how could it? The prime minister was careful to say little of his planning to anyone outside the cabinet, and in 1939 when, for example, the British began to consider an alliance with the Soviet Union in an attempt to check Hitler, King was furious, complaining bitterly to the British High Commissioner. How could any democracy hope to ally itself with the Communists? When Britain gave pledges of support to Poland and Rumania, King's response was almost the same, and he hinted that if such pledges led to war, Canada might not get involved. The British were never quite certain if they could count on Canada.

What is clear in all this is that Canada had no precise policy of its own, short of hoping for peace. Mackenzie King's Dominion really remained a colony, not an independent state. Canada played no part of any significance in the prewar manoeuvring, and none of the major actors on the world stage ever felt obliged to consult the Canadian government. The British counted on Canada or worried about it; they did not expect it to do anything other than to play a minor supporting role in the diplomacy of Empire. The Germans if they considered Canada at all, thought of it as a colony, one that would do its duty just as it had in 1914.

What then of independent nationhood? It existed scarcely at all, despite all the legalities erected since 1914 by Canadian prime ministers. If war came, Canada would go to war exactly as she had in 1914—because Britain went to war. There would be no other reasons of substance.

In a sense this was the greatest failure of King's career. He had been prime minister through the 1920s and for half of the 1930s. He had placed some substantial stress on his efforts to bolster a Canadian nationality. But he had done nothing of importance to give Canadians the right genuinely to decide for themselves on the major question of nationhood, the right to make war or to remain at peace. That question ultimately would be decided outside Canada, and all that Parliament would be able to decide upon was the scale of participation.

Conscription became an issue once again when Canada entered the war

But if King deserves to be criticized here, the country and its people can be faulted as well. Few in Canada wanted anything that smacked of real independence. There was no willingness or desire to be independent. Canadians were colonials and they received the leadership they wanted—and deserved. It would take the Second World War to change Canadian thinking, and Mackenzie King would change with it.

Chapter 4
War and Conscription

Maurice Duplessis campaigning

T he Second World War began in the early hours of September 1, 1939, when the German armies invaded Poland with massive force. For Britain and France, militarily unprepared as they were and essentially unwilling to fight, there seemed no way to avoid the struggle. Ultimatums to Germany expired on September 3, and the two great European democracies declared war.

For Canada, an ocean away from Europe, the Polish war meant that once again Canada would face a great crisis. War meant casualties, and casualties almost certainly meant that conscription would once again, as in 1917, become a divisive issue. Mackenzie King knew this as well as any man, and the prime minister was determined to avoid the issue if he possibly could. King's policy, therefore, was carefully framed. Many in French Canada opposed Canada's entry to war; they would have to be disappointed. Many in English Canada wanted a major war effort with conscription enforced instantly; they, too would be unsatisfied. The King policy was a balanced one. Canada would enter the war "at Britain's side," but Canada would not tear herself apart providing aid to the "last man, last dollar." Canada's effort would be limited to volunteers, to a large air effort, to all economic aid possible. The policy, in a phrase common at the time, would be one of "limited liability."

This was no forthright policy, no win-at-all-costs program. As

Top: Ernest Lapointe.
Lapointe was King's "French lieutenant."

Bottom: Mitchell Hepburn

Mackenzie King told the House of Commons on September 8 during its emergency session,

"I have made it...the supreme endeavour of my leadership of my party, and my leadership of the government of this country, to let no hasty or premature threat or pronouncement create mistrust and divisions between the different elements that compose the population of our vast dominion, so that when the moment of decision came all should so see the issue itself that our national effort might be marked by unity of purpose, of heart and of endeavour."

He had achieved this and there was scarcely a voice raised against Canada's entry into the war. King George VI signed the Canadian declaration of war on September 10. Canada and Nazi Germany were at war; six dreadful years would pass before peace returned.

The ink on the declaration was not dry before the fragile national unity was challenged in Quebec. Maurice Duplessis, the premier and leader of the Union Nationale, called a snap election, ostensibly on the issue that Ottawa was using the war to increase its powers at the expense of the provinces. To English Canadians, and to many in the King government, Duplessis's dissolution was an attempt to pull Quebec out of the war, something that had to be resisted with every effort.

Mackenzie King hesitated when his ministers urged him to permit federal intervention during the campaign, but in the end he went along. His closest colleague and the minister of justice, Ernest Lapointe, made a series of speeches throughout Quebec that had enormous impact. If you vote for Duplessis, the minister told his compatriots, all the Quebec ministers in Ottawa will resign. Then you will have conscription imposed on you by the English. If you reject the Union Nationale and elect a provincial Liberal government, then there will be no conscription. Lapointe's pledge was absolute, unconditional. And Quebec responded, massively rejecting Duplessis. The first threat had been overcome.

The second attack on King's national unity came from a different quarter—Ontario. The premier, Mitchell Hepburn, was a Liberal but, as he reminded his listeners on every occasion, he was not a Mackenzie King Liberal. To Hepburn, King was a coward, dragging his heels on the war effort, unwilling to help Britain. In the Ontario legislature early in January, 1940, therefore, Hepburn introduced a motion deploring that Ottawa "had made so little effort to prosecute Canada's duty in the war in the vigorous manner the people of Canada desire to see." The resolution, pushed through Queen's Park with the aid of the Conservative opposition, came like manna from heaven to Mackenzie King.

King signing the Commonwealth Air Training Plan in December, 1939

It was, King wrote in his diary, "just what is needed to place beyond question the wisdom of an immediate election and the assurance of victory for the government...it justified an immediate appeal..." With the resolution, King believed, he could have a quick election, and use the "damn the torpedoes, full speed ahead" Ontario attitude to good effect elsewhere in Canada where the government's cautious policies were appreciated. Equally important, King fully expected that the *sitzkrieg*, the non-war that prevailed along the Franco-German front in Europe, would come to an end in the spring. This, he wrote, was the greatest relief of all, "the probability of having the election over before the worst of the fighting begins in Europe...I have dreaded having to choose the moment for the campaign and specially to choose it at a time when human lives are being slaughtered by hundreds of thousands, if not by millions."

Parliament was dissolved on January 25, and the country plunged into an unexpected election campaign. It went exactly as King had expected. The opposition parties found themselves in disarray, the crowds cheered King's men to the echo, and everywhere there seemed to be a feeling of gratitude for the prime minister's policy of caution and limited liability. Even Conservatives found that appeals for conscription, big armies, a maximum effort, all stirred little positive response. There were too many Canadians out of work, too much of the Depression's effects still present for anyone to feel enthusiastic about fighting a war.

Mitchell Hepburn was one of King's most outspoken critics at this time. He accused the prime minister of trying to weaken provincial powers. King responded by appointing a Royal Commission to investigate the constitutional relationship between the federal and provincial governments. The Commission published the Rowell-Sirois Report in 1940.

The result of the voting on March 26 was a massive Liberal sweep, the largest electoral victory in Canadian history to that time. Mackenzie King won 181 seats, the Conservatives captured 40, and the Cooperative Commonwealth Federation only 8. Mackenzie King and the Liberal party were now securely in power for the next five years. On them would fall the responsibilities of the war.

Those burdens quickly became heavier as the *sitzkrieg* turned to *blitzkrieg*. In April, the Germans invaded Denmark and Norway; in May, Holland, Belgium, Luxembourg and France. Everywhere the *Wehrmacht* met with victory, driving the Allied armies back in disorder. The *panzers* swept all before them, and by the middle of June, 1940, France had fallen, Britain had been driven from the continent, and Hitler stood triumphant. For Canada, hitherto uninterested in the war, the turn of events had massive effects. Suddenly, Canada had become Britain's top-ranking ally.

The impact of the events in France and Flanders on the Canadian war effort was severe. Canada had sent one division of infantry (roughly 20,000 men) overseas in December, 1939. Further drafts were being prepared slowly. The country had agreed to pay some $350 million as the lion's share of the British

Top: Launching of the S.S. Victoria Park in October, 1942

Bottom: A Toronto Transit Commission float

Commonwealth Air Training Plan, a gigantic, cooperative effort to train pilots, bombardiers and aircrew of all types, largely in the open spaces of Canada. And the Royal Canadian Navy, a tiny force of men with only a few ships, patrolled the North Atlantic, escorting convoys and chasing away U-boats.

All this had seemed satisfactory to Canadians in the election of March, 1940. But once Britain seemed to be in danger of defeat, the national mood changed. In the House of Commons in May, Opposition members demanded Mackenzie King's resignation. Others called for conscription, and a vastly expanded war effort.

The government had to respond; indeed, the prime minister wanted to. But how to do it? French Canada still remained unenthusiastic about the war despite the collapse of the French republic, and conscription still stirred terrible memories of the past. After consulting with Ernest Lapointe, the minister of justice and the leading Quebec minister in the government, King decided on a measure that came to be known as the National Resources Mobilization Act. Hastily drafted, in large part by the prime minister himself, the N.R.M.A. gave the government sweeping powers to mobilize all the resources of the nation, powers that in fact were but a camouflage for the important clauses. For the Act permitted conscription for home defence.

C.D. Howe on a Victory Loan campaign in February, 1942

This was a neat tactic. French Canadians had always argued that they were not averse to defending Canada, far from it. Their objections were to being conscripted for England's sake and for English wars. Now, the government argued, Canada itself was threatened and now a home defence army had become essential. With little difficulty in the Commons and with only a few grumbles in Quebec, Parliament enacted the Act into law. The first bite at the conscription apple had been taken.

At the same time, war production began to increase dramatically.

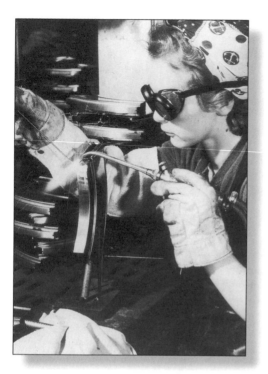

Woman welder, making guns for the war effort.

Few orders had come from Britain before the fall of France; now there seemed to be no end to them. In 1939 and 1940, war orders had amounted only to $310 million. The next year, the total was $810 million, and the year after, in a simply incredible increase, it reached more than $2 billion. The architect of this astonishing effort was Clarence Decatur Howe, an American-born engineer who had come to Canada to make his fortune and stayed to become one of the most powerful cabinet ministers in Canadian history. Howe operated like the tough businessman he was, pushing the laggards, giving good people their heads. The results were all that could have been needed. Tanks and planes, artillery, rifles, ammunition, raw materials and food—Canada produced everything, produced it well and quickly. Almost overnight the pall of depression was lifted and full employment existed everywhere. People had more money than ever before, and skilled labourers were the most wanted men and women in Canada.

How could all this be paid for? Taxes produced the bulk of the government's revenues, and the rates rose higher than ever before. Excess profits taxes governed the amounts that business could earn, and the government even imposed forced savings on wage earners. Additional money was produced by war savings bonds, and children saved their quarters for war savings stamps.

In fact, Canada became so wealthy thanks to the war that goods and war material were simply given away. Britain was the major beneficiary, and the English had to be. Their resources were so strained by the war that they simply could not pay for goods they desperately needed. And Canada had to produce the goods or see her wartime prosperity disappear. The solution was a gift of $1 billion in 1942, followed by mutal aid donations in similar amounts each year thereafter. By the war's end Canada had provided $3.5 billion in gifts to Britain and billions more in loans.

But despite this massive program of aid, many Canadians remained unhappy with the national effort. "How many Germans," one senior Conservative politician asked, "how many Germans have the Canadians killed?" What he meant, of course, was why was Canada's army not involved in the fighting? The army grew in size, eventually reaching five divisions in strength, and a total force of a half million men and women. But from 1939 to 1943, the bulk of the army sat in England, training endlessly. There were some adventures, but they were disastrous. Two thousand Canadians were lost at Hong Kong when the Japanese, entering the war in December, 1941, seized the island colony off China. And there was Dieppe. In one of the war's most brutal slaughters, 2,700 Canadians were killed or captured in a few hours of fighting in August, 1942. Whole regiments had died to test out the erroneous hypotheses of the planners.

Not until the summer of 1943 did the Canadian army begin to take an active part in continuous operations. One division helped capture Sicily, and another was added in the fighting in Italy. As they had in the Great War, the Canadian soldiers again proved themselves the equal of any in the world.

Still, people were dissatisfied. Canada needed conscription, some began to argue, if only for psychological reasons. Others said flatly that French Canadians were not fighting, that conscription had to be enforced to ensure that they did. There was some truth, but only some, in that last charge. English Canadians could and did get emotional about the war, about England. French Canadians couldn't and didn't, and for a Québécois to enlist required an effort of will and reason, not simply an emotional pull. Nonetheless Quebec enlistment's continued to be substantially higher than in the Great War, and the war effort put forward by the province was greater in all respects.

Hundreds of thousands of Canadians joined the armed forces and were sent overseas

J. Layton Ralston fought with King over the conscription issue and was fired by the prime minister

Few were convinced in English-speaking Canada, and in November, 1941, the Conservative party selected Arthur Meighen as party leader as a concrete expression of this disbelief. Meighen had served in Borden's Great War government, had drafted the Military Service Act, the conscription bill of that war, and had gone on to be prime minister for two brief spells in the 1920s. To Conservatives he was the embodiment of the vigorous war effort Canada needed; to French Canadians, he was the personification of Anglo-Saxon racism; to Mackenzie King, Meighen was the man he despised and feared.

Meighen's return to active politics made conscription again a political issue. In King's cabinet the minister of national defence began pressing for a larger army, supported by some of his colleagues. The press, particularly in Toronto, English Montreal and the west, began a vigorous crusade for compulsory overseas service. Questions were asked in the House of Commons. What was King to do?

The answer, the prime minister reasoned, had to satisfy English Canada but not offend Quebec. The answer was a plebiscite, a vote. The people would be asked if they wanted to free the government from its pledges made against conscription. To King, this seemed a clever stroke. It would get the question before the people in a relatively harmless way and free the government of its promises. It would get him a free hand without alienating French Canada.

But the prime minister had not banked on the depth of the opposition to conscription. French Canadians simply refused to contemplate the calling up of their men for overseas service in this war, and an extraordinarily effective pressure group, *La Ligue pour la défence du Canada*, sprang up to galvanize the opposition. The League played on the promises that had been made, stressed their binding nature, and urged Quebec to refuse to release the government from them. And it carried Quebec—72.9 per cent of the province—with it. English Canada voted "yes" on the plebiscite but King now was left with a worse dilemma than before.

The one saving grace was that Meighen was gone, beaten in a by-election in Toronto on February 9, 1942 by a C.C.F. school-teacher. That was some hope for the future. But now the problems came from within cabinet. Colonel J. Layton Ralston was the minister of national defence, and by 1942 he was very close to concluding that conscription would be necessary and that Canada should have it when it became so. Ralston drew his main support from Angus L. Macdonald, the former premier of Nova Scotia who had come to Ottawa at King's request in the summer of 1940 to become minister of national defence (Naval Services). The two strong ministers began to press their leader.

What had the plebiscite been all about if not so that conscription could be introduced, they asked King. What reason could there be for delay now? King fenced and stalled, hesitant and unsure. Any course seemed certain to alienate either English or French Canadians in the country at large, in the Liberal party and in his cabinet. Finally, in a brilliant feat of political balancing, he agreed to remove the clause in the National Resources Mobilization Act that permitted conscripts to be employed only in Canada. But he would not impose overseas conscription immediately, and possibly never. His ultimate policy, as he put it in a famous phrase, was "not necessarily conscription, but conscription if necessary." That sounded like double-talk, but in fact it expressed the government's policy exactly: the Liberal government would not necessarily impose conscription, but it would do so if and only if it became necessary. How to determine necessity was the problem.

Angus L. Macdonald wanted King to introduce conscription

Just how much of a problem became clear in October and November, 1944. By that date Canadian forces were heavily engaged in France and Italy. The Canadian army had landed in France on D-Day, June 6, 1944, and had participated splendidly in the heavy fighting around Caen, in the Falaise Gap and along the French coast. Casualties were heavy, and soon reinforcement shortages began to appear. It was not that there was a shortage of men; not at all. But there was a shortage of infantry, of trained soldiers. The generals had made their calculations, as they must, of casualties. They had estimated that more men would be killed and wounded in rear areas than was the case, and they had underestimated the numbers of infantry who would have to be replaced. By October, the minister of national defence, Colonel Ralston, had convinced himself that 15,000 more infantry were definitely needed.

Ralston had gone overseas to see the troops fighting in difficult conditions in Italy and in the Low Countries. He had heard stories of wounded men being returned to the front from their hospital beds

War and Conscription

Women's Army Corps recruiting in Winnipeg

because trained reinforcements were so scarce. This was too much for Ralston, a distinguished fighting soldier of the Great War, and a man who felt a deep and genuine personal responsibility for the Canadians who were fighting the war.

Ralston's return to Ottawa in mid-October, 1944, provoked one of the great political crises in Canadian history. On one side stood Ralston, a good, honest man who was fully convinced that if one casualty was incurred because of political considerations it was a crime. On the other side was Mackenzie King. He had no experience of war at the front, but he knew fully and well the effects war could have on a nation's unity. He had seen the wounds conscription had made in 1917. Who was correct? Who wrong? No one could answer that question in 1944; no one can answer it fully yet. The one certainty was that more infantry were probably going to be needed.

Where could they be found? There were 90,000 soldiers in

England and 120,000 in Canada who had volunteered to serve anywhere. There were also 60,000 N.R.M.A. soldiers in Canada, those men conscripted for service in Canada alone. According to the army staff, the 15,000 infantry could only be found among the N.R.M.A. men, not among the 210,000 other volunteers. The reasons were subjected to intensive examination and astonishingly enough, demonstrated to be largely sound. Only the home defence soldiers could be used.

For Mackenzie King, this was shattering. He had held off conscription for five years and now, with the war virtually won, he had to deal with it. He had the power to send the N.R.M.A. overseas; he had agreed that if it were necessary he would do so. But, King said, he had meant necessary to win the war. The war was already won; surely conscription was not really necessary now.

The cabinet fought and wrangled over the question for days, positions getting more fixed with every moment. Finally King, desperately trying to win time for his government, fired Colonel Ralston, and appointed in his stead General A.G.L. McNaughton, the former commander of Canadian troops overseas. A popular and democratic general, McNaughton did not believe in compulsory service, and he had convinced himself that he could find the men.

But three weeks later, McNaughton was a shattered man. His best efforts had produced nothing beyond being booed at public meetings, near disobedience from the generals and sullen non-com-

Churchill and McNaughton at British headquarters, 1941

Charles G. Power

pliance from the N.R.M.A. The generals told the minister that they could not find the infantry except in the N.R.M.A. and those soldiers would go overseas only if they were ordered. This was "a blow in the stomach," General McNaughton told King, and in one of the most astonishing turnabouts in Canadian politics, the prime minister suddenly and completely reversed his field.

Conscription had not been necessary before but now it was: "there is no longer thought as to the nature of the military advice tendered...it will be my clear duty to agree to the passing of the order in council authorizing the sending of N.R.M.A. soldiers overseas." The decision was made. King had fired Ralston because he wanted conscription; now he had to prevent his anti-conscriptionist ministers from resigning in protest at his introducing compulsory service.

A series of hurried telephone calls and meetings followed. Louis St. Laurent, Lapointe's successor as minister of justice, agreed to stay on, as did almost all the others. Only C.G. Power, an Irish-Canadian Quebecker and the air minister, believed King's decision wrong and left the government. But even here, King came off well. Power had gone because he opposed conscription, Ralston because he wanted it. Surely this meant that the prime minister was in the middle, a man of moderation, the man for all Canadians? This might have been a bit strained, but the idea seemed to take hold, and King survived, even carrying many of the Quebec M.P.s with him on a vote of confidence in Parliament. Whom else could they support after all?

The crisis ended with the government's decision to send 15,000 conscripts overseas where in fact they proved unnecessary. The Canadian sectors of the front were relatively quiet for the first months of 1945 and the reinforcement pools filled again; the Canadians in Italy were transferred to France, taking the men out of action for a breathing spell; and Hitler's Germany collapsed in ruins early in May. Only 2,463 conscripts found their way to the front by war's end, and, although they acquitted themselves well, their presence was essentially unnecessary. The Canadian war had been won with volunteers.

Those volunteers had paid a heavy price for their victory. The army lost 22,917 men killed; the navy 2,204; the air force 17,101.

Canadian women enlisted in the armed forces to help the war effort

Over 40,000 Canadians had died to stop Hitler, had died to rescue Europe from its follies.

For Mackenzie King, near exhaustion from the strain of the war, peace came as an enormous relief. He and his cabinet had run the war effort with unparalleled skill, harnessing the country's industrial power and mobilizing its manpower. In Canada there was continual criticism; abroad there was only praise. This country of ten million had acted like a great power in many fields and had established a reputation for producing the goods.

But to the prime minister, it had been a delicate balancing act. After the conscription crisis, he had stopped to reflect and write a few lines in his diary:

Over and over again I have thought...that some day the world will know some of the things that I have prevented... I must make increasingly clear to the world that prevention of wrong courses of evil and the like means more than else that man can accomplish. That lesson should be the one that comes out of the war.

This was no creed of dynamic leadership, but it was by no means incorrect in the Canadian context. In the war, King had prevented

Canadian soldiers in Ortona, Italy, 1943

national unity from being destroyed as it had been in 1917. He had prevented any serious reinforcement shortage overseas, and prevented conscription from destroying the country. He had prevented the opposition parties from coming to power, something that King would have considered a disaster beyond compare. And, cooperating with Canada's allies, he had prevented Hitler from winning the war. That was important above all and none could accuse Canada of slacking in this regard.

He had prevented a great deal, but King had accomplished much as well. Indeed, the war was Mackenzie King's most creative period. His foreign policy had made Canada a nation at last; his social policy had created a secure life for Canadians. That was something.

War and Conscription

Chapter 5
Peace and Security

No one would deny that Mackenzie King was a nationalist, a man who helped put Canada's independence on a firm foundation. Certainly King did this. But he was also a curious mixture of beliefs and attitudes in a way that, perhaps, is distinctively Canadian. To the prime minister, Britain was almost home. He admired the British, he loved, admired and revered the Royal Family, and he was proud to consider himself both British and an imperialist. But he disliked British policy on many subjects and he spent much of his political life fighting it.

The Americans were viewed in almost the same way. King admired the energy of the United States, its force, its capabilities. He was probably as close to President Franklin Roosevelt as he had ever been to any foreign leader. But he feared the power of America, and he was well aware that as a small nation Canada had to be exceedingly careful to avoid falling under American control.

What was the best policy for Canada in these circumstances? Before the war, King had tried to stay aloof from the events of Europe. He had used his links to the south as a way of counterbalancing the efforts from London to drag Canada into a closer embrace. But circumstances could alter, and when they did, King would change with them.

King with his dog at Kingsmere during the war

And the circumstances changed with stunning rapidity in 1940. From being a great power at the head of a vast Empire, Britain was suddenly reduced to the position of a struggling survivor, desperately fending off the power of Hitler's Germany. From being a wealthy state, Britain was reduced to borrowing and begging the materiel and munitions she needed to stay alive. And by the next year, the United States, brought into the war by Japan's attack at Pearl Harbor, was clearly the coming power in the world. The wealth, industry, and

Peace and Security

global reach of the Americans ensured this.

How could Canada survive in this changed state of affairs? Mackenzie King did what had to be done. Although at no time did Canada stint on giving aid to Britain, the nation nonetheless set in train a series of links with Washington.

The first such link was the Ogdensburg Agreement of August, 1940. In that month Britain was at the nadir of her power, and few really expected the island nation to survive. For Canadians, this meant that closer links with Washington were essential. Essential so that Canada could survive if Britain did not; essential so that as much aid as possible could be given England from a Canada that did not need to worry over its own future or its own defences.

With this in mind, Mackenzie King went to the small northern New York town of Ogdensburg to meet President Roosevelt, who was in the area doing some election campaigning and reviewing troops. Roosevelt was smiling and benevolent, and he proposed the creation of a Permanent Joint Board on Defence, to link together the defences of the two great North American states. King did not hesitate for a moment. He agreed readily and the agreement was fact.

The Defence Board established by the two leaders became a functioning reality in a few weeks. Studies were launched, defences strengthened and, for the rest of the war, Canada had no need to look to her own security. Of course, the American presence could sometimes get too close for total comfort. By 1942 the United States had about 15,000 troops in Canada working on the construction of a highway to Alaska and a string of airfields and other installations. Too often, the United States authorities forgot to ask permission for these privileges; but although there were some who called the Americans "the army of occupation," matters could usually be sorted out. However, the lesson was clear—you had to tread carefully with your best friends too.

The next formal link with Washington came in April, 1941. By this time in the war, Canada was feeling the economic pinch. Britain could no longer pay for the goods she needed and, in order to produce these goods, Canada had to import more from the United States. This meant that Britain owed Canada millions while Canada owed Washington millions more. How could it all be brought into balance? The answer, Mackenzie King quickly came to realize, was to persuade the Americans to buy more in Canada. If this were done then the trade books would come into balance, Canada could help Britain better, and the war would be won in the quickest and most economical fashion.

This was King's intent and he went off to see Roosevelt once more. At Hyde Park, the President's home in New York State, the two men met on a "grand Sunday in April" for a long talk.

Roosevelt had said to King [Grant Dexter, a reporter from the *Winnipeg Free Press*, wrote confidentially after a talk with Mackenzie King] *that he didn't know much about the exchange situation: that he would like King to tell him about it and outline the policy which Roosevelt should follow. King hadn't bothered about the economics of it. He told Roosevelt that if he were in his place he would have regarded (sic) only for the neighbourly phase of it. What the U.S. and Britain had done was one thing. Canada as the neighbour on this continent, the only one that really mattered, was another proposition entirely. If the U.S. insisted on taking from Canada what few possessions she had in the U.S. it would only give voice to anti-U.S. sentiment in this country. Why not buy from Canada as much as Canada is buying from the U.S.—just balance the accounts. Roosevelt thought this was a swell idea.*

It may not have been quite that simple, but the problem was resolved with dispatch. Canada's fiscal difficulties with the Americans were resolved, and aid to Britain could increase at the same time as Canadians grew more prosperous. The cost to the United States was negligible.

King, Roosevelt, and Churchill, at Quebec, 1943

Everyone gained, or so it seemed. But by the end of the war the economic and industrial links between the two countries were so close, so intertwined, that many thoughtful Canadians wondered if Canada could ever break free. King had set the country on a course that integrated it with the United States. But had there been any choice? Had there ever been any choice?

At the same time, King continued to resist British efforts to treat Canada as a fourth-rate colony. The British took the aid from Canada as their due, asked for more, and assumed that no say on matters of importance to Canada need be given the Dominion in return. This is no condemnation of the British—all great powers act the same. But to Canadians, to Mackenzie King, it was infuriating. At the time of Ogdensburg, for example, King had been convinced that he had helped save the free world by dragging the still-neutral Americans into a closer relationship to the belligerents. Prime Minister Winston Churchill, however, had grumped and complained, and King was crushed.

King's relationship with Churchill was an interesting and curious one. Before the war, he had considered the British politician an irresponsible warmonger, a positive danger to peace. But once Churchill came to power in the dark days of May, 1940, once the great speeches began to galvanize Britain, King's attitude altered. Churchill now was a great man—as indeed he was. But he was still an imperialist of imperialists, someone who had to be watched lest he drag Canada into commitments that would destroy the independence that the war was bringing to the fore. There was a tension in King's relationship with the British leader, no affection to speak of between them, and a good deal of mistrust.

London's unwillingness to recognize Canada's new industrial and financial power did not make the King-Churchill relationship any easier, nor did the continuous efforts Churchill's government made to prevent the Dominion from securing a place on British-American boards and agencies. It was all so frustrating to the Canadian prime minister, trying to help win the war and trying to put Canada into a proper position befitting her new strength.

The answer was a now-forgotten doctrine called functionalism. King expressed it in a speech in July, 1943, when he said that "authority in international affairs must not be concentrated exclusively in the largest powers." Representation on world agencies "should be determined on a functional basis which will admit to full membership those countries, large or small, which have the greatest contribution to make to the particular object in question..." Where Canada had the resources and skills and power to act as a great nation, in other words, she demanded to be treated as one. And those areas of Canadian power included food, raw materials, and the potential for civil air transport.

This principle did not win ready acceptance from London, Washington or Moscow, all seats of the Great Powers. But simply to express the functional principle was to give notice that Canada could not readily be dismissed. Simply to utter it was to foster Canadian independence and nationalism. And there could be no doubt whatsoever that the Canada that emerged from the war was vastly different than the nation that had entered it in 1939. Then the land was wracked with economic disease; in 1945 there was a full boom. Then the factories had produced few manufactured goods in relative terms; in 1945 the country was a giant. Then the total federal budget was a tiny $600 million; in 1945 it was around $5 billion. The Gross National Product had doubled in six years and every one of the economic indicators showed huge increases. This power, this new power, was the basis for the Canadian claims.

Equally important, the Canadian people had a new confidence in their nation and in their government, a direct result of the vast systems of social security that the King government had launched. It is worth recollecting that in 1939 there was no unemployment insurance, no family allowances, no Canada pension plan, only an old age pension that required a humiliating means test before giv-ing recipients a pittance. There was no security for any but the rich, and the Depression had made the people's situation worse.

The war, paradoxically, provided the opportunity to change things round. In the midst of the killing and waste of war, and in part at least because of it, Canadians and their government changed the way they lived.

The first great measure was unemployment insurance. This had been talked of for years and Prime Minister Bennett had passed a bill for unemployment insurance in 1935, only to see the courts reject it on constitutional grounds. Mackenzie King wanted it, too, but the provinces were not all in favour. Carefully and slowly he worked on them until by early 1940 all were in line. As King said of the measure, "Authorities in the field...are generally agreed that the most favourable time for its establishment is a period of rising employment during which time a fund can be built up out of which benefits can subsequently be paid." The war provided the opportunity. If, as everyone feared, with peace the Depression might again settle on the land, unemployment insur-ance could cushion the shock. The bill became law in the summer of 1940 and King was delighted with his role:

Two new political parties had been born during the Depression, partly as a protest against the Bennett government's failure to cure the country's economic ills. Top: J.S.Woodsworth with the parliamentary caucus of his Cooperative Commonwealth Federation (C.C.F.).

This is really a great achievement for the Liberal Party...For all time to come that will remain to the credit of the Liberal Party under my leadership. It was when I was nominated leader that the party for the first time committed itself to this particular reform.

That first commitment had been in 1919, of course, and thousands and thousands of the unemployed had suffered without insurance through the 1930s. Never again.

But after that great measure in 1940, there was a long pause while all energy focused on the war. Mackenzie King paid little attention to events at home except conscription, so absorbed was he in the war. It was, therefore, with some shock that he suddenly realized in 1943 that the political scene had altered completely.

The first to change were the Conservatives. After their failure to put Arthur Meighen into Parliament, the Tories had set out on a rebuilding course. They had decided correctly that they were seen as reactionary, and in consequence they had changed their image. It was, therefore, as the Progressive Conservative party with a progressive leader in John Bracken, the long-time premier of Manitoba, that the Tories set out to fight for votes. The new party platform, adopted at a great convention in Winnipeg in December, 1942, called for social welfare and promised a human society for every Canadian. In one leap, the Tories had jumped into the centre of the political road.

On the left, the Cooperative Commonwealth Federation was booming. The C.C.F. had beaten Meighen in Tory Toronto by talking social welfare. Flushed with success, the party never looked back. Membership rose across the land. By-elections began to be won regularly, and in August, 1943, the C.C.F. won 34 seats in an Ontario provincial election, coming from nowhere to form the Opposition. The next year the government of Saskatchewan would be captured and a national Gallup Poll even showed the C.C.F. leading the old parties in September, 1943. The future seemed to belong to the C.C.F.

For King and the Liberals, there was a feeling of injustice in all this. Here the government was winning the war and neglecting politics while the Opposition were cleaning up at home. It did seem unjust, but King had one great advantage. He was in power and he could enact measures while the other party leaders could only make promises. And act King did.

William Aberhart, leader of the Social Credit movement

After a Liberal conference in 1943 had laid the groundwork, the government's Speech from the Throne opening Parliament in January, 1944 spelled out the government's plans. The "postwar object of our domestic policy is social security and human welfare," the governor general read. "The establishment of a national minimum of social security and human welfare should be advanced as rapidly as possible," and the government promised to guarantee useful employment for all, to upgrade nutrition and housing and to provide social insurance. A generous and fair deal was promised to returning veterans and a panoply of new government departments was created to administer the brave new world.

It was a great program, one that King's whole life had been aimed at, and the prime minister now began to carry it out. One of the most important measures was family allowances, introduced in Parliament in June, 1944. This "baby bonus" bill proposed to pay to mothers $5 a month for each child. The intent was that the money would be used to improve nutrition, to buy proper clothing for the

King laid the foundations of the Canadian welfare state by introducing the old-age pension, unemployment insurance, and the family allowance.

young. Critics charged that the money would be squandered on alcohol or luxuries; others claimed that Ottawa was giving money to large French-Canadian families when those very French Canadians would not fight in the war. But in fact, as the government figures demonstrated, Quebec got substantially less than people believed, and Ontario, the province with most complaints, both got more and was helping support the west, not Quebec.

The family allowance scheme would cost about $250 million a year. This no longer seems like such a huge sum, but in 1939 the total federal budget had only been $600 million. Almost half of prewar spending was now to go to one program. Nor does the $5 per child any longer seem like much. But in the war years the average wage was under $25 a week, and $5 seemed a fortune. In fact, when the government tried out the baby bonus scheme in Prince Edward Island early in 1945, many people refused to believe it—it was too good to be true. Well, it was true, and it changed Canadian life. It also helped keep Mackenzie King and the Liberals in power.

This last was naturally part of King's intent, but only part. The real reason for family allowances and all the other social security schemes that started in wartime was to put money into circulation in peacetime. The great fear of government economists was that a depression would return once the war orders dried up. The million men and women in the armed forces would come home, find no jobs, and revolution (worse than the Winnipeg strike in 1919) would sweep the land. How could this be prevented?

One way was to put money in people's pockets, money that could and would be spent. This would create a demand for goods, and this would keep factories producing. If the plans faltered, then the state would create jobs through massive public works projects, by building dams and bridges, planting forests, opening up the North. All this sounds simple and commonplace today, but it marked a revolution in economic and government thinking, a change in the role of the state.

And it was with this policy that Mackenzie King went to the voters in June, 1945. He had won the war, he could make the peace, and he had ensured the security of Canadians. This was an effective program to put before the voters, particularly as the C.C.F. could be portrayed as socialists, as people in too much of a hurry, while the Tories were easily painted as reactionaries masquerading as progressives. King was in the middle, the man for all seasons. And the people

[Opposite]
V-E Day in Toronto

Mackenzie King broadcasts a message to Canada on V-E day, May 8, 1945

responded, re-electing Mackenzie King's government. This was the triumph of his life—to be re-elected after six years of war and hardship. Even Winston Churchill, the saviour of Britain, was promptly tossed from power at the war's end. But not Mackenzie King.

I sat quietly for a short time in the sunroom [King wrote after getting the results of the election], *in my heart thanking and praising God for his goodness. The relief of mind that I experienced is indescribable...I felt a real vindication in the verdict of the people and the sense of triumph therefrom.*

Mackenzie King had fought his last election.

Peace and Security

Epilogue: End of a Life

Mackenzie King would govern Canada for three years after the end of the Second World War in 1945. The old man (and he was seventy-one in 1945) hung on to power, for he realized that power was all he had. Still a bachelor, still a nearly friendless man, to give up office was almost to give up life.

The last three years were not easy ones. The country had to be led through the process of conversion to peace. All the controls built up to run the war effort had to be dismantled gradually. The machinery of government had to be scaled down and life returned to normal.

King congratulating St. Laurent at the swearing in of the new prime minister. Viscount Alexander, the governor general, is at centre.

But it quickly became evident that nothing would be normal again. In September, 1945, a cipher clerk named Igor Gouzenko fled from the Soviet embassy in Ottawa carrying with him proof of a widespread spy ring run by the Russians in Canada. Links to spies in Britain and the United States were found, and the Cold War began. An atmosphere of suspicion, never absent during the war among the Allies, now grew all-pervasive. Trust was gone and the preparations for the next war were in hand before peace had any chance to become established.

For Canada, geographically situated on the shortest air route between Moscow and Washington, this was a matter of grave import. And the country had no doubt of its course, of its duty in this new crisis. Canada had learned the lessons of appeasement in the 1930s and this time it would be different. King's cabinet, and particularly his secretary of state for external affairs, Louis St. Laurent, were firm believers in collective security, in an alliance directed against what they saw as aggressive communism.

The "ruins" at Kingsmere

The prime minister, however, remained cautious and skeptical. He was no friend of the Soviets, but he worried about the Americans and British, too, and he exercised all his powers to restrain his colleagues. But by 1947-48 King was old and tired, worn down by years of carrying the burdens of government. He had no strength for the kind of cabinet fight he would have waged earlier, and St. Laurent and the others got their way on most things.

Indeed, St. Laurent, the Quebec lawyer who had served in the cabinet since 1941, was King's choice for his successor and, at a carefully managed (but open) convention in August, 1948, the torch was passed. Under the new prime minister, Canada would join the North Atlantic Treaty Organization in 1949 and send troops to fight in Korea in 1950. The policy of no commitments, the constant refrain that Parliament would decide, had ended.

Mackenzie King would live for only two more years. The old man puttered among his flowers at Kingsmere in the Gatineau hills near Ottawa, or sat among the artificial ruins he had constructed there. He had hoped to write his memoirs but his energy had drained away. On July 22, 1950, he died. His last words, said to a nurse leaning over his bed, were "thank you."

What are we to make of Mackenzie King? He was never a popular figure—indeed he might even be the most disliked of our prime ministers. His policies are remembered for their cunning and trickery, his speeches for their sanctimonious platitudes and built-in escape hatches. He made the Liberal party what it is today—a party with room for everyone, a party that governs without fixed principles, a party that rules adequately and for long periods of time.

King was no hero, no dashing figure. But somehow he gave Canadians what they seemed to want. And what they wanted was a man who did not divide them. King did not. He kept the country together, a difficult task. They wanted a leader who did not threaten them with rash adventures. King's caution was ready-made for soothing fears. They wanted a leader who cared about them. Mackenzie King was not a poor man, but he did care for his people, and he created a society that gave a larger share of the good life to all than had been the case in the past.

This was King's real achievement. The country he found when he came to power in 1921 was a rich one with wealth inequitably divided. An individual made it or failed; there seemed no middle ground. The country he left to his successors was still one with great inequities, but now the state threw its weight onto the scales, redressing somewhat the balance between rich and poor, between the few and the many. Everyone was entitled to a share, unequal as it may have been, of the country's wealth.

And King had used the war to achieve this. He had also done great things in this period, too—actions that outweighed the policy of inaction and small government he had seemed to symbolize in the 1920s and 1930s. During the war, King and his government had mobilized the people and resources and produced a simply superb war effort. He won the war, as much as any Canadian can be said to have done so. He kept racial tensions down, balancing issues and personalities, fighting for time and ultimately opting for the correct courses when time ran out. His achievement in the war stands unchallenged as the greatest effort of political statesmanship by any Canadian prime minister. All one need do is compare the scandals and divisions of the Great War to the splendid record from 1939 to 1945 to see the magnitude of his achievement.

Mackenzie King was a great prime minister. He was unloved and he will remain unloved because he was not a great man. But his flaws of personality should not obscure his achievements. They were great and lasting; they made Canada what it is today.

Igor Gouzenko's face was never photographed for newspaper stories about the trial, and he appeared in court wearing a hood.

William Lyon Mackenzie King

1874	Born in Berlin (later Kitchener), Ontario, on December 17.
1895	Attends University of Toronto and later does post-graduate work at University of Chicago.
1897	Publishes articles on sweatshop conditions in Toronto *Mail and Empire*.
1900	Becomes editor of the *Labour Gazette* and is made deputy minister of the newly formed department of labour.
1908	Wins seat in Parliament and is named minister of labour.
1909	Completes doctoral degree in economics at Harvard.
1911	Loses seat when Liberals are defeated by Conservatives under Sir Robert Borden.
1914	Becomes labour relations expert for the Rockefeller Foundation.
1917	Liberals are defeated again, this time over the conscription issue.
1918	*Industry and Humanity* is published.
1919	Becomes leader of the Liberal party.
1921	Liberals are victorious and King becomes prime minister.
1925	Liberals lose general election but King refuses to concede defeat.
1926	Introduces old age pension. Resigns when governor general refuses to dissolve Parliament at his request. Wins a general election after Meighen dissolves Parliament.
1929	Stock market crashes on October 24; Great Depression begins.
1930	R.B. Bennett's Conservatives defeat the Liberals, putting King out of office.
1935	Liberals returned to power with a huge majority.
1939	King promises Canadians there will be no conscription for overseas service in the event of a war in Europe. Canada declares war on Nazi Germany on September 10.
1940	Government passes Unemployment Insurance measure. Liberals win largest electorial victory in Canadian history. King introduces National Resources Mobilization Act (N.R.M.A.) allowing conscription for home defence.
1942	Holds national plebiscite on conscription issue.
1944	Reverses his stand on conscription and agrees to send M.R.M.A. recruits overseas. Introduces "baby bonus" (Family Allowance Act).
1945	World War II ends. King is re-elected prime minister for the fifth time.
1948	King resigns and Louis St. Laurent becomes prime minister.
1950	Dies on July 22 at Kingsmere and is buried in Mount Pleasant Cemetery, Toronto.

Further Reading

Dawson, R. MacGregor. *William Lyon Mackenzie King.* Toronto: University of Toronto Press, 1948. Volume 1.

Gray, Charlotte. *Mrs. King: The Life and Times of Isabel Mackenzie King.* Toronto: Penguin, 1998.

Gray, James L. *The Winter Years.* Toronto: Macmillan, 1966.

Hutchison, Bruce. *The Incredible Canadian.* Toronto: Longmans Canada, 1970.

King, W.L.M. *Industry and Humanity.* Toronto: T. Allen, 1918.

King, W.L.M. *The Mackenzie King Diaries, 1932-1949.* Toronto: University of Toronto Press, c1980.

Neatby, H. Blair. *The Politics of Chaos.* Toronto: Macmillian, 1972.

Nolan, Brian. *King's War: Mackenzie King and the Politics of War, 1939-1945.* Toronto: Random House, 1988.

Power, C.G. *A Party Politician.* Toronto: Macmillan, 1966.

Stacey, C.P. *A Very Double Life.* Halifax, NS: Goodread Biographies, c1985.

Wardhaugh, Robert A. *Mackenzie King and the Prairie West.* Toronto: University of Toronto Press, 2000.

Credits

Every effort has been made to credit all sources correctly. The publisher will welcome any information that will allow it to correct any errors or omissions.

Manitoba Archives, pages 41 (John E. Parker Coll. 19, N8468), 44 (Canadian Army Photo Coll.162, N10857)
Ontario Archives, page 5
National Archives of Canada, pages 6 (C-046506, C-007332), 7 (C-002853, C-007318), 8 (PA-074737), 10 (C-028574), 11 (C-046521), 12 (C-000932), 14 (C-021314), 17 (PA-028136), 19 (C-005799), 23 (C-009064), 26 (PA-052387), 27 (C-020594), 28 (C-014162), 29 (C-030305), 32 (C-055372), 34 (C-029452), 36 (C-024720, C-019529), 37 (C-024696), 38 (C-030761, PA-054039), 39 (C-019380), 40 (C-7481), 42 (C-013257), 43 (PA-047435), 45 (PA-119399), 46 (C-013252), 47 (C-053595), 48 (PA-114030), 49 (C-020049), 51 (C-014168), 54 (PA-167544), 55 (C-009339), 56 (C-023268), 57 (RD-000887), 58 (C-022716), 61 (PA-129625, *Montreal Star*)
Toronto Public Library, pages 3, 13, 21, 24, 35, 59, 60, 63
United Church Archives, page 9

Index